FIRED, LAID OFF OR PUSHED OUT?

. . .

*A Handbook of Strategies for Saving
Your Neck When The Ax Falls At Work*

Jonathan P. Arfa

Copyright © 2013 by Jonathan P. Arfa
All Rights Reserved

Printed In the United States of America

ISBN: 1480044377
ISBN 13: 9781480044371

All contents are original and do not infringe upon the legal rights of any other person or work. Contents and/or cover may not be reproduced in whole or in part in any form without the express written consent of the Author.

'I'm sorry, but business is slow and the company is going through retrenchment. Your position has been eliminated'

• • •

'There doesn't seem to be a position for you in the firm's future plans'

• • •

'As the new manager, I want to put my own team in place and there isn't a place for you'

• • •

'Remember those stock options we used to induce you to leave the secure, cushy job you had?'

• • •

'Uh Oh! Don't look now, but those options are no longer worth the paper they are printed on and you're out of a job!'

Acknowledgements & Thanks

The author would like to express his deep gratitude to the following who contributed their time, opinions and critiques to the manuscript (alphabetically):

Rob Clarfeld, C.P.A., CEO/President, Clarfeld Wealth Strategists and Financial Confidantes ™

Josephine Linden, Linden Global Strategies

Peter Post, Managing Partner, Roth Post Advisors

Kenneth Simendinger

Kathleen G. Strickland, Principal, The Strickland Group, Ltd.

My thanks as well to others who do not wish to be individually identified for their contributions and to Ali Pepe who assisted in manuscript preparation.

• • •

And a big thank you to my wife, Dr. Barbara Bernstein, daughter, Meredith A. Arfa, Esq. and my son, Benjamin Arfa for their thoughtful comments and support.

TABLE OF CONTENTS

Preface	1
Part One	7
Setting The Stage	7
1. Why Is This Happening To Me?	8
2. Getting Started	16
3. First Step – Gathering Your Facts And Documents	21
3.1. Documents Concerning The Recruitment ProcessAnd Pre-Hire Period	22
3.2. Documents Concerning The Period Of Active Employment	25
3.3. Documents Concerning Your Termination	26
3.4. Relevant Information	27
4. Second Step – Identifying The Key Players	31
4.1. Your Spouse/Life Partner	31
4.2. The Employer	33
4.3. The Recruiter	35
5. Third Step – Finding And Hiring A Lawyer	39
5.1. What Kind Of Lawyer Am I Looking For?	39
5.2. Different Types Of Lawyers	40
5.3. How Do I Find The Right Lawyer?	42
5.4. How Do I Recognize The "Wrong" Lawyer For Me?	43
5.5. What To Expect From The Consultation	44
5.6. How Much Detail Should I Expect (Want) From The Lawyer?	47
5.7. What If I Have No Case?	48
5.8. What If My Rights May Have Been Violated?	48

6.	Third Step Continued – Establishing A Fee Arrangement With Your Lawyer	50
	6.1. Hourly Fee Arrangement	51
	6.2. Straight Contingent Fee Arrangement	54
	6.3. Blended Hourly and Contingent Fee Arrangement	56
	6.4. Flat Fee	63
	6.5. Reducing The Fee Agreement To Writing	63
	6.5.1. What To Include In An Hourly Fee Arrangement	64
	6.5.2. What To Include In A Contingent Fee Arrangement	66
	6.5.3. Taking Tax Considerations Into Account	71
	6.5.4. Defining When Legal Fees Are Payable	73
	6.5.5. What About Disbursements And Expenses?	73
7.	"JUICE - I" Leverage vs. Risk	75
8.	"JUICE - II" The Economics Of Risk & Reward	85

Part Two   96
How Much And What Kind Of Leverage Do You Have?   96

9.	Termination Of The Employment Relationship	97
	9.1. The Employment At-Will Rule	97
	9.2. Exceptions To The At-Will Rule	100
	9.3. Why Do I Need To Think About This?	101
10.	Deals & Agreements	103
	10.1. The Written, Fixed Term Agreement	104
	10.2. Verbal Deals And Agreements	109
	10.3. Employer Promulgated Rules	113
11.	Statutorily Created Rights	117
	11.1. A Word About The Discrimination Laws	120
	11.2. Other Types Of Statutory Claims	123

12. Public Policy Considerations	124
13. Constructive Termination	125
Part Three	126
Moving From Theory To Action	126
14. Getting Ready To Negotiate	127
14.1. Choosing Your Negotiating Posture	128
14.2. The "Aw C'mon" Approach	131
14.3. The "Stick-Em Up" Approach	131
14.4. Are "Aw C'mon" And "Stick-Em Up" Inconsistent?	132
15. "Aw C'mon" Negotiations	134
15.1. Who Should Do The Negotiations?	136
15.2. The Risk of Getting Lost In The "Group"	138
15.3. Your Place In The "Food Chain"	138
15.4. Leveraging Your "Aw C'mon" Appeal To The "Max"	139
16. "Stick-Em Up" Negotiations	142
16.1. Damages: Leverage Involving A Contract Claim	143
16.2. Damages: Leverage Involving A Discrimination Or Tort Claim	146
16.3. "Juice" May Be Illusory	147
16.4. Talk Is Cheap: An Employer May Do It For Strategic Reasons	149
17. Getting In The Front Door or "Can We Talk..."	151
17.1. The "Do It Yourself" Negotiator	151
17.2. Using A Lawyer To Be Your Negotiator	152
17.3. Selecting The Initial Contact	154
17.4. Deciding Upon The Method Of Initial Contact & The "Demand Letter"	157

18. Once You're In The Front Door	162
18.1. Type I: Small Employers That Are Sure That They Have Done Nothing Wrong	163
18.2. Type II: Larger Employers That May Not Care	164
18.3. Type III: Larger Employers That Do Care	166
19. Getting Down To Negotiating	168
19.1. Securing Sufficient Time Within Which To Consider Your Employer's Initial Offer	169
19.2. Ambivalent Negotiating Stance: Problems With "Testing The Waters"	171
19.3. Strategy Relating To Contract Claims	174
19.4. Computing Damages If You Have A Viable Claim For Violation Of Your Statutory Rights	177
19.5. The Value Of Settlement	179
19.6. Prioritizing Your "Wish List" Items	181
19.7. The Different Negotiating Stances	185
19.8. The "Hard" Bottom Line	186
19.9. The "Soft" Bottom Line	188
19.10. Diagrammatic Examples of "Bottom Line"	190
Part Four	**193**
Done Deal....Almost	**193**
20. The Separation Agreement	195
20.1. What Am I Missing: Agreement Basics	195
20.2. General Rules To Guide Your Negotiations	198
21. Getting Started: General Rules Of Contract Interpretation	207
21.1. The Role Of The Judge In Deciding Your Lawsuit	207
21.2. The Overriding "Main Purpose" Rule	209
21.3. The Plain Meaning Rule	210
21.4. Lawful, Effective and Reasonable Interpretations Are Preferred	210

21.5. Taking Circumstances Existing At Contract Formation Into Account	211
21.6. Ambiguities Are Construed Against The Drafting Party	211
21.7. "Usage Of Trade"	212
21.8. Omitted Terms	212
21.9. The Parol Evidence Rule	213
22. Non-Financial Terms Of Settlement	214
22.1. The Parties	214
22.2. The Nature Of Separation	215
22.3. The Date Of Termination	218
22.4. The Release	223
22.4.1. Mutual Or Unilateral?	224
22.4.2. Release vs. Termination Of Obligations	228
22.4.3. Exceptions, Exclusions & Carve-Outs To The Release	230
22.5. Indemnification & Defense	234
22.5.1. Defense	235
22.5.2. Indemnification	236
22.6. Non-Competition And Other Restrictive Covenants	239
22.6.1. No-Solicitation Of Employees	241
22.6.2. No-Solicitation – Customers And Accounts	245
22.7. The Non-Competition Provision– General Considerations	248
22.7.1. The Non-Competition Provision – The Impact of Termination on Enforceability	252
22.7.2. The Non-Competition Provision – The "Employee Choice Doctrine"	253

- 22.7.3. The Non-Competition Provision – The "Unique Employee Doctrine" ... 254
- 22.7.4. The Non-Competition Provision – The "Inevitable Disclosure Doctrine" ... 255
- 22.7.5. Consequences Of Former Employer's Attempt To Seek Injunctive Relief ... 257
- 22.8. Confidentiality ... 260
- 22.9. The Non-Disclosure Provision ... 264
- 22.10. The "No Derogatory" Statements Provision ... 267
- 22.11. The Successors and Assigns Provision ... 269
- 22.12. Unemployment Insurance ... 271
- 22.13. References ... 273
- 22.14. Miscellaneous Provisions ... 274
  - 22.14.1. Miscellaneous Provisions: The Zipper Clause ... 274
  - 22.14.2. Miscellaneous Provisions: Severability ... 276
  - 22.14.3. Miscellaneous Provisions: Choice Of Law, Forum & Venue ... 279
  - 22.14.4. Miscellaneous Provisions: Waiver Of Re-Employment Rights ... 282
  - 22.14.5. Miscellaneous Provisions: Transitional Assistance And Advice ... 283
- 23. Financial Terms Of Separation ... 289
  - 23.1. Earned Compensation ... 289
  - 23.2. Bonus or Incentive Compensation ... 291
  - 23.3. Severance And Salary Continuation ... 293
  - 23.4. Deferred Compensation ... 301
  - 23.5. Vacation ... 304
  - 23.6. Sick/Personal Leave ... 305

23.7. Pension And Retirement Plans	306
23.8. Health And Medical Insurance	307
23.9. Outplacement	312
24. Getting Ready To Sign The Agreement	318
Afterward	321

Preface

Your vacation is planned, but not yet paid for. The kids are off to camp. You're thinking about a new car because the current lease is almost up. You plan to do some home renovations when you have a little bit bigger financial cushion. You have resigned yourself to working for more years than you had planned because your retirement account isn't what it used to be. Given what has happened over the last number of years in the economy and the job market, you have a more realistic perspective. Life isn't grand, but it's not bad either.

WHAM! You are called into the human resource director's office and are told that you are being let go. What about the vacation and new car? Your first thought is how can this be happening? You've been a star employee for years; your performance evaluations have been good or better. You get regular raises. Your colleagues and co-workers aren't going to believe this. You are sure that everyone is going to be shocked. This is so unfair!

• • •

No matter how it is said, nor whatever nicety is used, being told that you are about to lose your "job", and therefore your livelihood, hurts. Even the word "job" is inadequate for many employees, executives and highly compensated individuals. After all, it's not just a "job" – with it may go your status in your industry; your status in the community in which you live; your spouse's status; your income stream; your financial and emotional security; and your well-planned future. The loss of employment places all of those factors, and more, in play.

It is a basic truism that the involuntary loss of employment is almost never anyone's first choice. That said, however, loss of employment – particularly at senior levels – no longer carries the stigma that it once did in the latter decades of the twentieth century. More recently, employees at virtually all levels in the American workforce, and executives in particular, are constantly in motion. Workforce reductions and realignments are commonplace and have reached epidemic proportions in some industry sectors. Employment in today's global economy bears virtually no relationship to the days of the World War II generation of workers who spent most of their working careers with a single employer.

While various legal nuances may apply to the different ways in which a loss of employment occurs, the practical bottom line is the same. The job that provided you and your family's income stream and financial security has, or is about to come to an end. Psychologists and career counselors say that the loss of employment ranks right up there among life's worst crises and places a great strain on you and your family. Count on it!

Exactly what you call your loss of employment, therefore, is fundamentally irrelevant (*e.g.* I have been fired, laid off, "RIFFED", excessed, become redundant, etc.). Moreover, how you "spin" your loss of employment should be clearly distinguished from the *manner* in which a termination is effected and the way in which it is managed by you and your employer. It can make all the difference if you and your employer can work together to manage the separation in an attempt to significantly mitigate the impact. Going into a tailspin with the corresponding failure, or inability, to manage this process can only exacerbate matters.

Well planned and carefully executed transitional management can be a "win-win" for both you and your employer. But if not well managed, a transition can be a nightmare for you with potentially long lasting consequences even though it rarely becomes a nightmare for your employer.

This is not the time to freeze and rush into crisis mode; there's plenty of time for self-recrimination ("I should have seen the handwriting on the wall") later. No, this is the time for a clear, well thought through plan of action – in business school parlance, a business plan. Your personal business plan should be as well developed as any other business plan or model you would create for your employer. Only now, it's personal.

One final introductory note: unfortunately, the law is not good at second guessing legitimate (even if misguided, unfair or wrong) management, personnel and business judgments. The law also generally stays clear of pronouncements on a company's moral and ethical standards and lapses. Thus, rights, strategy and leverage are the name of the game. Your moral outrage, or even the genuinely felt indignation of your peers, subordinates, colleagues, friends and relatives, just aren't worth all that much – at least in terms of dollars in a separation package. They may help salve your wounds and generate sympathy, but that's for another day.

▶ **What This Handbook Is**

This Handbook is your roadmap through the process of separation. The optimal end-game is a separation package that cushions your transition (and perhaps does even more), ultimately leading to your re-employment, comfortable retirement or new career. This Handbook deals with the practical "how-tos". It starts, and ends with the assumption and expectation that no one reading it should confidently fly solo and decide to navigate on your own. That is what distinguishes you from other employees who lose their job – you know better than to diagnose and treat yourself. And you have taken the first step by reading this Handbook.

Much of what you will learn and discover while reading this Handbook should also be instructive for you as you transition from your former job to a new position. That includes an understanding as to what documents you should retain, notes that you should make, and contractual provisions, rights and protections that might be appropriate for you to negotiate on your way into a new position. The experience of the things that did and did not work well for you in the separation process can be quite useful as you navigate into a new job.

To the extent that you are unable to obtain the level of contractual comfort you seek from a new employer, it nevertheless is useful to appreciate the degree to which you are at risk when entering into a new relationship without such protection so that you are better prepared if things don't work out. More about this towards the end of this Handbook.

▶ *What This Handbook Is Not*

This Handbook is not designed to give you legal advice and it certainly does not have the answer as to why you have lost your job. If you are an executive or other highly compensated employee, you are unique for your sophistication. You understand process and numbers. And you understand strategy. Other, less senior employees, may not be quite as business savvy. Those readers should rely more upon the expertise of others. Regardless of who you are, however, it is never as easy to do for yourself those things that you may have successfully done for others over the years or, perhaps, never done before.

It's now time to take a deep breath and start the process of preparing your personal business plan for transition. This Handbook provides you with the basic tools required to formulate, fine-tune and execute your personal business plan of action.

• • •

A final note: I have used the words "he", "his" and "him" throughout this Handbook for continuity of writing rather than switching between male and female references. Of course, all references apply equally to male and female and all such references can be read interchangeably.

Part One

Setting The Stage

Either your employment has been, or you anticipate that it is about to be terminated. You are not sure what to do and you are anxious about the future. You may have been offered severance but are required to sign an agreement that contains a lot of legal language and provisions that are foreign to you. You do not know the significance of some of the provisions in the agreement your employer has presented and you are not sure whether the agreement is okay for you to sign. You feel that the severance and benefits offered to you in exchange for signing the agreement are inadequate and you think your rights may have been violated. The situation is even worse when your employer has terminated your employment and not offered you any severance pay or benefits at all.

This Part of the Handbook sets the stage. It discusses how to develop a personal business plan to get you through the process of separation. It outlines how to choose a lawyer, identifies the key players in the negotiation process, and addresses how to evaluate the amount of leverage you may bring to negotiations to get a severance package or increase the package already offered by your employer. It provides a roadmap of how to prepare to meet with a lawyer and finally, it provides guidance as to how to weigh the potential upside of negotiations against the downside risks.

1.

Why Is This Happening To Me?

If you are reading this Handbook, you likely fall into one of the following categories:

- ▶ You have a solid reason to believe that your employment is about to come to a screeching halt – probably involuntarily; or

- ▶ You have just been notified that your employment is being involuntarily terminated for unspecified "business" reasons; or

- ▶ You have just been notified that your employment is being involuntarily terminated, effective immediately, for "misconduct", "cause" or based upon some specific allegation of wrongdoing; or

- ▶ You have just been notified that you are heading toward involuntary termination but you have been given a 'grace period', or reprieve of several months, in which to remedy performance deficiencies identified by your employer; or

▶ The decision to terminate your employment has already been made but you have been given some time in which to find alternative employment before the termination becomes effective; or

▶ You have just been notified that your employment is being involuntarily terminated, and you were told to clean out your desk and was unceremoniously shown to the front door (and maybe have been introduced to an out-placement counselor retained by your employer to assist in the 'transition'); or

▶ You are going to lose your job and have decided to exercise a "retirement" option rather than try to re-enter the workforce and seek new employment; or

▶ No one has said anything to you yet, but you see the handwriting on the wall and want to get ahead of the curve and negotiate a voluntary exit strategy.

If you were surprised when you were told that you are going to lose your employment, management may not have done its job in properly communicating with you all along. Or you may have missed or ignored management's signals. Or you don't read the trade journals or newspapers or watch the news. Or your company is in far more critical financial shape than management has been letting on.

While it may be hard to see now, there is a light at the end of the transitional tunnel. In fact, once you arrive at the other end, you may well find that the transitional process – as terrible and unwanted as it was – has enhanced your ability to manage your career and left you in a better position to evaluate your worth in the marketplace. Rarely does an employee look forward to an involuntary loss of employment. Unfortunately, it has become a common fact of life. In retrospect, many employees believe that they not only survived the ordeal, but find that they are on a new course which holds even greater potential and security for them and their family. As it often unfolds, the unknown is not nearly as confounding as it at first seems.

Dr. Elisabeth Kübler-Ross's seminal book, *On Death & Dying*, published in 1969, is a worthwhile read into her pioneering methods in the support and counseling of personal trauma associated with death. Kübler-Ross's ideas, notably the five stages of grief (denial, anger, bargaining, depression, acceptance), are instructive and transferable as well to the personal change and emotional upset that results from loss of employment. Before you start down the transitional path from employment, to unemployment, and back to gainful employment, the following bears noting. In fact, repeat it out loud:

IF THINGS LOOK AND FEEL LOUSY NOW, HANG ON: THEY WILL LIKELY LOOK AND FEEL WORSE BEFORE THEY GET BETTER.

But, if history is any guide – and those who have gone through it will tell you that it is – ultimately, things will look and feel better. It takes time, calm and careful strategic planning and some positive market conditions. Planning for the transitional period and beyond is really just another business puzzle that you encounter throughout your career. Only the stakes are higher because this is personal.

In order to successfully navigate this transition, you must prepare a game plan – the previously referenced personal business plan. You may have created business plans on a routine basis as part of your job – even if you did not formally identify them as such. Or, you may have been part of a team that executed your employer's business plan. Now it's time to prepare a business plan for yourself. Whether you have done this before or this is new to you, the basic components are the same: identify the goals, risks, rewards, options and alternatives, and end-game.

▶ *What's My "Story-Line"*

As a preliminary matter, it is valuable to try and identify the reasons behind your separation. Often, it is no secret – you are told directly by management. Business is off; your performance is below target; the business unit is being acquired, merged or consolidated; a newly hired, more senior employee wants his/her own team; you have been accused of engaging in a specific act of misconduct; or, sometimes, management just needs a sacrificial employee.

An understanding of your employer's motivation will assist your transition strategy in one critical way.

This knowledge will better enable you to explain the separation to a prospective employer. It goes without saying that it is easier to explain a loss of a job to a recruiter who has read about lay-offs or a management/workforce reshuffling at your firm in the business newspapers or on-line reports than it is to explain rumors of your personal misconduct such as an allegation of sexual harassment.

You certainly want to make every effort to be sure that whatever you tell a prospective employer is consistent with what your employer will say by way of press release, SEC or other regulatory filing, litigation filings, employment references and otherwise. Misrepresentation in an interview, or in a resume, is a recipe for disaster and should be avoided at all costs. Misrepresentation, however, should be distinguished, from "spin" – or putting the most favorable face on an otherwise unattractive story. An outplacement professional or other career advisor or coach, headhunter or employment agency professional should be able to help with that.

▶ What If I Say That I "Resigned"

Employees often view "resignation", or a statement announcing that you and your employer have reached a "mutual decision to go our own ways", or that you are leaving your position to "spend more time with your family", as a cure-all. But it is unrealistic to believe that you can successfully rely upon an explanation that your separation was "purely voluntary" in order to avoid answering difficult questions concerning the reasons for the separation. This is especially true in flush labor (buyers) market when it will not ring true to a recruiter or hiring professional that you have voluntarily left your employment before having secured a new job. Employees do not tend to leave themselves naked in that manner and it is difficult to sell that kind of explanation.

The same is true with the "I decided to take some time off between jobs to find myself" explanation. Bite the bullet; try to get an agreement from your employer for a reasonably neutral explanation for your separation and then "spin". Indeed, an integral part of any negotiation with your employer should include an understanding as to what your employer will tell third parties concerning the reasons for your separation and by whom. While the issue may have no immediate, demonstrable cash value, the manner in which the issue is handled may make the difference between a short and long transitional period –- and that may have cash value.

Many employers have adopted a policy that they will only confirm dates of employment and perhaps the last position you held. If that will be your employer's response to an inquiry concerning your employment, it will provide some – but not total cover. The more senior you are, the more likely it is that a personal contact will be made by senior people at your prospective employer with a colleague at your former employer who may be more willing to share "off the record" information. As a result, you should not assume that your employer's *pro forma* statement concerning your termination will necessarily be the only information that you will have to deal with.

▶ How Do I Handle Termination For Personal Misconduct

Where your termination involves some type of actual or alleged wrongdoing on your part, it is critical to try to become conversant with the specific allegations and evidence that the employer has compiled concerning the claims. Sometimes, that's not very easy. Your employer may be concerned about creating a claim such as defamation or wrongful termination where one did not already exist. Moreover, absent litigation, you generally have no right to receive answers to these questions.

Nor do you have a right in most jurisdictions to access to your employee personnel file, copies of complaints against you or reports of internal investigations conducted by your employer. It is possible that you may be entitled to the results of an investigation conducted by an outside entity under applicable federal or state litigation discovery rules. As a result, it is critical to seek independent professional advice concerning the legal consequences of the alleged conduct so that you can attempt to protect yourself against possible post-employment legal entanglements.

The most significant areas of potential exposure involve conduct relating to financial improprieties and claims of personal wrongdoing such as improper physical contact, embezzlement or sexual harassment. The last several years have made it apparent how difficult it is to hide allegations of wrongdoing. Corporate America (with significant nudging by Congress, state legislatures and outside watchdog groups) has become far more aggressive in vetting all kinds of conduct that had not historically been treated as a major issue. Employer efforts to sanitize the workplace has made even seemingly innocuous conduct become grounds for action by an employer.

The risk of entering the marketplace to seek new employment without being armed with this information can dramatically increase the risk that hearsay and rumor will take on a life of its own. If that happens, you may not be in a position or be prepared to respond properly or timely. Nothing makes a candidate for employment less attractive than a cloud of financial, sexual or other improprieties. That is especially true in a "buyer's market" where there is an abundance of qualified applicants. However, even where this happens, the game is not lost. But it should emphasize the importance of preparation and strategic planning.

As a result, deferring or avoiding the distasteful, but necessary process of self-evaluation and delving into the motives behind your termination can be costly. You should avoid starting the transition process with one hand tied behind your back. The more information you collect, the better equipped you will be to deal with whatever comes down the road.

Moreover, just because your employment relationship with your company ends, this does not mean that the underlying issues of wrongdoing have also reached an end. Many such issues can survive your termination and may continue to cause you such problems as ongoing litigation in which you may be named a party or be called as a witness long after you have left the company's employ. Investigations, depositions, litigation, trials and the like can be very time consuming and costly. They can also make finding and keeping a new position more difficult.

2.

Getting Started

Before putting pen to paper (or pounding the keyboard), the principal question you need to resolve at this preliminary stage, is what you optimally want out of the unwanted process of separation. The answer is not always clear. In fact, don't be surprised if your initial, visceral assumptions change after you have a chance to get some fresh air and some time and space to clearly think things through. In other words, goals and aspirations often look different after several good nights' sleep and a healthy dose of reality check – along with some time to acclimate to your new, uncertain future. The development of a personal business plan forces you to prioritize the things that you want and to weigh each against your evaluation of the likelihood of success in attaining your goals. Doing so allows you to fine-tune your plan *BEFORE* you enter the contested arena of negotiations with your former employer.

Employees often are reluctant to aggressively pursue their self-interest just because they are losing their job. In times of low unemployment, a seasoned executive may legitimately believe that he likely will be re-employed in short order. While that may turn out to be true, blind reliance on that assumption risks serious miscalculation. Moreover, in difficult economic climates and during periods of high unemployment and downbeat or uncertain economic indicators, such an assumption is likely to be far from reality. It is tautological that in such times, the job market shrinks. Even for highly skilled, well regarded executives. As a result, the job market can become particularly treacherous and driven by economic uncertainty along with domestic and international turmoil. Companies are likely to be resistant to hire until well after the economy rebounds and consumption increases in order to reduce the company's risk of guessing wrong.

Thus, and in difficult economic times, the goal of the separation process may be more heavily weighted toward financial considerations than might be the case in a tight, seller's job market.

▶ *It's All About the "Benjamins"*

After all is said and done, the bottom line of virtually every transitional personal business plan – no matter how you dress up the various considerations – largely involves, and can be reduced to: "how much can I get". Some separating employees are shy about couching their goals in these stark financial terms. Others profess to take the high road: "I want to leave with my integrity intact", or "I don't want to burn any bridges" or "I understand what the Company is doing and why." Nice sentiments, but if you are able to negotiate a significant severance package, that may temper the cost of burning that bridge or walking away with your integrity between your legs. The bottom line almost always is about cash and other financial benefits.

Most separating employees crave moral vindication. They often seek to ratify their own view that the termination is unfair, or not their fault, or how stupidly or irrationally their employer is behaving. However, regardless of how much you may want it, moral vindication generally is elusive. And, except for any possible short-term personal gratification you may experience, moral vindication is not all that valuable an asset and may come, if at all, at a disproportionately high price.

An exception may be public vindication after a trial if you have been accused of some type of personal wrongdoing or misconduct and you win the case. But even here, the cost in time and resources to get a public vindication may still turn out to be disproportionate to any value added.

Your personal business plan should provide the roadmap to your carefully defined end-game: maximizing the cash and benefits you negotiate on separation. Your business plan should identify where you are, how you got there, where you want to end up, and the options you can identify for getting there.

▶ *Putting Your Plan On Paper*

While your plan does not need to be in writing, making notes and columns of "pros" and "cons" and "pluses" and "minuses" often prove helpful. Forcing yourself to reduce your thoughts to writing not only imposes needed discipline, it often has a cathartic effect. Doing the numbers can be a real eye opener. Often, you are more secure financially than you thought; sometimes, however, not nearly so much – the pool of retirement dollars (and your house) that you have counted on may have suddenly dropped dramatically in value – especially if you have a large portion of your assets in the stock of the very employer that is now causing your separation because of a need for financial retrenchment. It's a classic double whammy. Not only is the company's financial condition causing you to lose your job, it has also cut the asset value of your 401k, retirement plan benefits, deferred compensation or various equity awards that you have been counting on.

In sum, the discipline required to develop a sound, comprehensive personal business plan is designed to slow you down so that you are forced to intelligently think through your situation rather than make rash, unrealistic moves.

Your success at meeting your transitional goals requires a realistic understanding and evaluation of the leverage (*"JUICE"*) that you can bring to the process: do you have it and, if so, how much! You can't buy *JUICE*; and you generally don't inherit it. *JUICE* comes from being in a stronger position – actually or perceptively – than the other side. It comes from having more leverage than the other side and it comes from properly assessing that leverage and from knowing how to strategically use any *JUICE* you may have.

Every successful business person is a closet expert on *JUICE*. You may not know it, but you have already honed the fine art of the use of *JUICE*. That's how you became successful in your job. It also is a skill that you will have to draw on in order to successfully negotiate your separation. *JUICE* is taught in business schools everywhere – that's how important it is to successful negotiations. It may carry a more formal course number or even a more high-powered course title, but the course content is the same: *JUICE*: where to get it and how to use it.

• • •

▶ Should I Take It, Leave It, Or Negotiate

This is the point at which you should decide whether you are satisfied with the terms of separation that you have been offered by your employer. Or, even if you are not satisfied, whether you would rather take the offering and walk away than fight for more.

Alternatively, are you prepared to pursue an intermediate (moderate although aggressive) path of negotiations short of all-out battle?

The rest of this Handbook addresses the process of negotiating with your employer. If you have elected either immediate battle (head straight to the courthouse and file a lawsuit) or just want to walk away, stop here. If you are going to take the offering without trying to negotiate better financial terms, go directly to Part 4.

For the rest of you, let's get started.

3.

First Step – Gathering Your Facts And Documents

If you have not yet decided whether to sign any agreement presented to you by your employer (or walk away without looking back if you have not been offered anything), you will want to consult with a lawyer. You should do this for one or both of the following reasons.

First, you should get advice as to what an agreement presented by your employer means to you both legally and practically.

Second, you may want a professional evaluation of the circumstances surrounding your termination in order to determine whether any of your legal rights might have been violated. In addition, the lawyer can assist you with identifying your options and deciding how to proceed.

In order to make your initial session with a lawyer as productive as possible, you should assemble all of the documents and information that are relevant to each phase of your employment relationship.

Some of this information may be too old or stale to be relevant, and the lawyer will quickly identify and disregard such information. If you are not sure, include the document. As a general rule, it is better to assemble more documents than you think you might need then it is to be missing a key document that you thought was unimportant. In addition, you should make a note to tell the lawyer about documents you know once existed but which you do not have. You should also prepare a written chronology of relevant events during your employment and those related to your termination. The more detail the better – it may not all be useful, but your memory of events will dim as time goes by.

The following categories contain sample lists of documents and information that you should assemble in advance of your consultation with the lawyer. Of course, these lists are not exclusive and if there is something you think might be important, you should include it. A note of caution: since you are exploring your legal rights which could conceivably lead to some type of litigation, you should preserve documents of all types that you have (e-mails, letters, memos, notes, etc.) that might in any way relate to your employment or any claim you might assert against your former employer. These documents may be subject to production in discovery if the matter ends up in litigation and you could be subject to significant penalties if you have discarded any such documents.

3.1. Documents Concerning The Recruitment Process And Pre-Hire Period

- ▶ your diary, planner or calendar for the relevant period which indicate the dates, times, places and persons with whom you interviewed;

- ▶ notes made by you during, and following each interview;

- ▶ notes made by you during, and following each telephone call you had with the recruiter and each company representative;

▶   copies of benefits booklets, employee handbooks, pension and retirement plans (or the Summary Plan Descriptions), and equity plan documents provided to you during the interview phase;

▶   introductory or firm marketing booklets given to you by the recruiter;

▶   annual reports and similar corporate filings and booklets prepared by the prospective employer;

▶   correspondence, including e-mails, from the recruiter to you and copies of such communications to the prospective employer relating to you as a candidate;

▶   correspondence from the prospective (and now former) employer that discusses the company, its benefits, the position for which you are interviewing and general terms and conditions of employment enjoyed by the company's new hires;

- business cards from employees at the company to whom you were introduced, or with whom you interviewed;

- notes and records that reflect any other job solicitations received by you during this pre-employment period as well as any interviews and offers of employment that you received or were pending during this period;

- notes reflecting discussions that you had with individuals formerly employed by the company who you contacted for further background and information relating to the company, the position for which you were interviewing, etc.;

- copies of drafts (and transmittal e-mails) of any offer letter and employment agreement exchanged during the negotiation phase leading up to your acceptance of employment.

- the final offer letter, term sheet or employment agreement.

3.2. Documents Concerning The Period Of Active Employment

- ▶ all documents that reflect an amendment or modification to your initial hiring letter, employment agreement or contract;

- ▶ copies of all drafts and final versions of subsequent and new agreements;

- ▶ copies of all amendments to benefits plans, booklets, employee handbooks, pension and retirement plans, and equity plan documents;

- ▶ annual and other performance appraisals, reviews or evaluations;

- ▶ letters, in-house newspaper or bulletin articles commending or otherwise commenting upon your performance by the employer;

- ▶ letters and other types of documents from customers or other third parties attesting to, or commending your performance;

- letters, memoranda and other documents that are critical of your performance;

- documents that contain goals, expectations, or performance benchmarks and all documents that reflect your employer's view of your performance against such standards and goals;

- records of your compensation and benefits including salary, bonus, 401K, equity awards, automobile allowance, club membership, etc.;

- records that indicate the corporate identity of the firm that employed you, paid you, and provided benefits to you (which may not all be the same).

3.3. Documents Concerning Your Termination

- your diary, planner or calendar which reflect the dates, times, places and persons who spoke with you concerning your termination;

- notes made by you during, and following each conversation concerning your termination;

► computer printout, benefit statement or other type of chart that reflects your benefits, options, stock and equity grants etc. along with the vesting and exercise status of each;

► current news reports or articles that relate (directly or indirectly) to your separation;

► SEC and other filings that relate to a specific corporate transaction that is driving the termination;

► SEC and other filings that report or disclosure your termination;

► all agreements, cover/transmittal letters from the employer to you offering any type of separation benefits.

3.4. *Relevant Information*

In addition to documents, it will be useful to the lawyer if you are able to gather some of the following information:

► Information as to whether the termination of your employment is individual to you (*i.e.* not part of a larger restructuring or downsizing), and, if so, what you "hear", "have been told" or "guess" is driving the decision.

- If your loss of employment is part of a larger, broad based downsizing or consolidation, it would be useful if you are able to provide specifics as to what the demographic makeup of the affected workforce both before and after the separations.

- If the termination is purportedly part of a restructuring or downsizing, your thoughts as to whether the articulated business justification for the downsizing or reorganization makes business sense to you and, if not, why not.

- Alternatives to the termination of your employment that were available to your employer in connection with a restructuring that would have impacted you less (or not at all).

- Information as to whether you have been, or are you going to be replaced and, if so, by whom (and the more information about the sex, age, race, national original etc. of the replacement the better).

- How your qualifications, experience and performance stack up against the individual replacing you.

- The Company's view of the financial considerations that may have played a role in your selection for separation.

- How the salary that was being paid to you compares to the market salary for individuals in your industry with the same or similar job.

- Whether the rest of your compensation package is in line with market.

- Whether fringe benefits are a disproportionately large part of your total compensation package.

- The discretionary/variable parts of your compensation package, if any, and the amounts of each.

- Cost savings that can be expected by your employer from your separation (short, medium and long term).

- Whether separation benefits are a direct charge to your department/division's P&L or payable out of an off-line budget.

- Information concerning the details of both historical and current separation packages offered to colleagues or peers at your firm.

Don't be concerned if you cannot locate certain documents or information, even if you are sure that you once had them. It is as important for the lawyer to know and review the records and documents that you are able to assemble as it is for the lawyer to know what you no longer possess, but recall once having. It also is important for the lawyer to know what records and documents may never have existed.

Take the time to put the documents and information in some sort of useful order (chronological; by category, etc.) before your meeting with the lawyer. It will save significant time during your initial session and reduce the need to flip through a pile of documents to look for the one sheet of paper that you are certain you brought, but just cannot locate immediately.

If you have consulted with a lawyer prior to, and in anticipation of losing your employment, get some guidance from the lawyer as to what you should put in writing and how/whether such writings might be protected (not subject to discovery) by the attorney-client privilege.

4.

Second Step – Identifying The Key Players

As with any business plan, a key element of your personal plan is to identify the players who have been, or will be important during each step of the process. They may include members of your family, outside professionals, recruiters, employers, friends and colleagues. Here, we address two players who certainly will be important: your spouse/partner, and your employer and a third player who may be important – the recruiter. A fourth key player, the attorney, is discussed in the next 2 chapters.

4.1. *Your Spouse/Life Partner*

Before you start down the path of ex-employee survival, a note concerning your spouse or life partner – perhaps the ultimate *player*. You should disregard whatever role your spouse or life partner may (or may not) have played in your business life up to this point. That's history and should not serve as the benchmark for the amount of involvement this person can, or should have during this transitional phase. Even a spouse who has been wholly uninvolved in the day-to-day particulars of your business life will necessarily assume a different role during this transitional period.

You should allow for the strong possibility that your spouse may have exaggerated fears and concerns about his or her future social status and financial security, as well as the reaction of family and friends to your loss of employment. It is not unreasonable to have a general unease about what the future may hold. And don't let your partner's 'happy face' fool you. The unknown is often frightening just because it is the unknown. News reports of people being unemployed for many months can be unnerving.

You may even find that while you are spending more time at home re-discovering the pleasures of free time, you also are interfering with your spouse's daily routine. You should further allow for the possibility that your greater physical presence is not always quite the blessing to others that you assume it is. Everyone needs some time and space; while yours has been externally and involuntarily imposed on you, your spouse does not have to be an additional victim.

Thus, your spouse/life partner becomes perhaps the most important player during the entire transitional period. Not only can your spouse be a source of support and comfort to you during this difficult time, but your spouse may also become an interim (and perhaps enduring) source of income and support for the family unit.

Your failure to fully embrace your partner throughout this journey increases the risk that your relationship may not survive intact. As a result, you may also lose the surest source of aid and comfort unconditionally available to you when you need it most. Machismo in the boardroom, or in the executive suite, or "on the desk", or in the office may have worked well for you yesterday. But this is today, and at least during the transitional period, you have been consigned to work outside these centers of the universe. Take full advantage of your partner's availability and expertise – two heads often are better than one in working through this process.

4.2. The Employer

Your employer certainly is a key player. Some would argue that the employer is the ultimate player. The reason should be obvious. It was your employer that made the decision to hire you and then terminate your employment. It holds the keys to your severance and benefits and its conduct can significantly impact your search for new employment.

There are several considerations relevant to developing a negotiating strategy with your employer. You are probably in the best position – at the worst time – to evaluate each of these considerations. Preliminarily, you should attempt to evaluate whether you are generally viewed favorably by those in senior management with decision making authority concerning your separation package. In doing so, you should evaluate the extent and nature of your personal relationship with those decision makers (*i.e.* do you have a reservoir of good will that can be called upon; will they go to bat for you; were they directly involved in the decision to hire or fire you).

Good will may be critical to successful negotiations with your employer. In fact, good will can sometimes carry you further in negotiations than great lawyering; conversely, where there is no such reservoir of good will, aggressive legal posturing may be the best available option.

Each company has its own institutional culture and constraints that will guide its approach to negotiations with you. As recent press reports indicate, there may be heightened sensitivity as to how senior management, the company's Board of Directors (or compensation committee), stockholders, legislators, regulators or the press may view payment to you of a sizable separation package. It is important to consider these potential concerns so that you do not overplay your hand and, where possible, strategize how to provide cover for the company. Your lawyer should be able to advise you concerning the company's obligations to publicly disclose all or part of your package under various SEC and other regulatory reporting and disclosure rules.

Your knowledge of the corporate players and the way in which the company has dealt with other separating employees also is important. This information may provide a baseline as to what you might expect, and it may also be useful to point to these examples as precedent during negotiations. Don't be surprised if your lawyer tells you that these prior instances have no legally significant precedential value. While that may be true, such instances may nevertheless provide the company with a defensible reason for accommodating you. Management generally does not want to be a trail-blazer, especially when parting with corporate largess during difficult financial times. It may need a good reason to do so.

While your employer controls the purse strings, your skill at devising a sound, strategic negotiating plan may determine how far open you can pry the corporate purse. At its core, it's all about your effective exercise of leverage – your use of effective negotiating skills as a means to achieve an end. You can count on your employer to do the same.

4.3. The Recruiter

The recruiter's role in the pre-hire process leading up to your acceptance of employment with your employer may be important and deserving of evaluation. The recruiter's role is probably most relevant where the time between recruitment, hiring and termination is fairly short. If not, intervening events may render the recruiter's conduct during the pre-hire period largely or wholly irrelevant. If a recruiter was not involved in placing you in your job, skip this section.

Often you can re-construct your interactions with a recruiter by reference to your diary, correspondence, e-mails and notes taken by you during meetings and conversations with the recruiter. You should do so.

As a bottom line matter, the recruiter's role is that of paid match-maker. The recruiter's function is to identify outstanding, qualified candidates to fill a job vacancy that has been placed with the recruiter by a corporate client. Unlike an employment agency, the recruiter generally initiates contact with prospective candidates and solicits interest from prospects. Sometimes the referral of a potential candidate comes to the recruiter from another executive with whom the recruiter has worked. Other times, the recruiter may have had direct contact with a candidate in the past who seems ideally suited to fill a current search. Less often, the recruiter finds a candidate as a result of cold-calling or, perhaps, as a result of candidate identification by its corporate client (*i.e.* the company has a specific candidate in mind but, for a variety of reasons, wants to use an intermediary to make the approach and solicitation).

It is important to remember that recruiters are almost always compensated for their services by their corporate client. Fees generally are a percentage of the successful candidate's annual compensation. Thus, the recruiter usually earns no fee unless, and until, the recruiter identifies and delivers the successful candidate. This can vary with those recruiters who are on a retainer, search or annual fee basis with their corporate client. Nothing angers a recruiter more than finding a candidate who successfully completes all pre-employment screening and interviewing and is offered the job by the recruiter's corporate client, only to have the offer bested by the candidate's current employer, or by another company with which the candidate is also interviewing.

Recruiters, as a class, are no different from other groups of professionals. Many are excellent at what they do. They view a successful employment marriage as more than just an opportunity to earn a fee. Rather, they view their role in the process as an integral link between the ultimate corporate consumer and the selling executive universe. Good recruiters will not attempt to force a marriage; they are fully aware that ultimate satisfaction by both their corporate client and the executive they have placed is likely to yield business dividends in the future.

On the other hand, there are some recruiters motivated primarily by the short-term financial gain to be made by making a placement. It is these recruiters that are more likely to 'finesse' the details of the available position and overly embellish such points as duties, responsibilities, lines of reporting and supervision, compensation, benefits, promotional opportunities and the company's financial picture.

During the initial contact with you, the recruiter may only have identified the position for which it was seeking candidates without identifying the corporate client on whose behalf the recruiter was conducting its search. It did so in order to preliminarily gauge whether you had any interest in the position, particularly if its corporate client is making a confidential search. As with most match-makers, the recruiter's initial pitch probably placed a favorable spin on the position for which it is recruiting candidates and, sooner or later, its corporate client. Sometimes, it is difficult to separate legally meaningful representations and promises made by the recruiter during the early stages of the recruitment process, from flowery salesmanship of hope, hype, anticipation and aspiration.

The distinction, however, may be critical. While it is incumbent upon a candidate for employment to exercise a degree of independent due diligence by investigating the claims and factual assertions made by the recruiter, it should be obvious to anyone who has been through the recruitment process that you are likely to experience only limited success in obtaining advanced, full disclosure. Indeed, it often is only after a position has been offered, accepted and employment actually begun that the recruiter's 'puffery' becomes clearly distinguishable from reality.

The degree to which you are able to accurately reconstruct the recruitment phase of your relationship with your former employer will drive the ability of your attorney to differentiate, in legal terms, the 'puffery' from the potentially meaningful 'representations', 'promises', 'guarantees' and 'assurances'. The former generally carry no legal consequences; the latter may involve a viable legal claim against either the recruiter or your former employer, or both. The extent to which you used reasonable due diligence to try and verify the factual landscape painted by the recruiter may be important in assessing the legal consequences that might flow from a recruiter's overly creative presentation.

For purposes of legal analysis, the recruiter may be an 'agent' of its corporate client. As a result, and if the acts of the recruiter were legally wrongful, such acts may be independently actionable and/or attributable to the recruiter's corporate client.

5.

Third Step – Finding And Hiring A Lawyer

The fact that you are reading this Handbook likely means that you have concerns about the circumstances, manner or reasons your employment has been (or is going to be) terminated. You also probably want to know whether there is a way to "shake money [or more money] out of the severance tree".

5.1. What Kind Of Lawyer Am I Looking For?

While it should go without saying, you should consult with and, if indicated, retain only a competent attorney licensed to practice law in your state with a specific, in-depth knowledge of and expertise in employment law. Your friend, cousin, friend's friend or general family attorney will not do.

You should no sooner consult with the attorney who drafted your last will and testament than you would consult with your childhood pediatrician for some adult ailment. The law governing employment relationships is complex and requires someone with particular expertise in this area. Be cautious of the lawyer who professes expertise in multiple legal disciplines – he may know a little about a lot, but not a lot about your area of concern.

The attorney wears several hats. He is your counselor, advisor and confident. He is an expert who can identify whether you have any legal claims arising out of the termination of your employment. He may also be your strategist and lead negotiator.

5.2.   Different Types Of Lawyers

Every attorney approaches each case and client from a somewhat different perspective and with their own strategic sensibilities. Moreover, each attorney brings a different life experience, legal training, practical legal experience and sometimes, a definite philosophic bent. As a result, you should not hesitate to consult with more than one attorney before deciding upon which attorney to hire since there often is no single correct approach.

Thus, the "shark" may be a top flight lawyer, but not the right lawyer if you are seeking a softer, low-keyed approach. Some lawyers are publicity hawks; they love to see their name (and, if they are lucky, their photo) in print. A high profile lawyer may seem to fit the bill, but that genre of attorney might also cause more harm than good. And, of course, cost may be a consideration.

If you are a senior executive, you probably have had frequent exposure to attorneys during the course of your day-to-day business affairs. To the extent that you have a personal relationship with your company's corporate counsel, that attorney may seem like a logical first place to turn, either for advice, or for a recommendation of an attorney with specific employment law expertise. Regardless of the relationship you have with your company's corporate counsel, however, you should communicate with the company's counsel quite judiciously.

Your company's corporate counsel has – and can have – only one client – your employer. Whatever the company counsel's personal opinion may be with respect to you or your situation, counsel's duty of loyalty runs first and only to your employer. Thus, by consulting with corporate counsel (even "off-the-record"), you may place counsel in the position of acting against the best interests of his client (your employer) or place him in an untenable position if you disclose information that counsel feels compelled to disclose to the company or feels ethically obligated to act on. Either way, you may prejudice yourself.

Moreover, corporate counsel may end up representing your employer with respect to any claims asserted by you regardless of the personal relationship that you had with counsel beforehand. After all, "it's just business – nothing personal"! There are strategic considerations that you should review with the lawyer you ultimately hire as to whether the company's counsel should be barred from representing your employer on the basis of a conflict of interest arising out of counsel's relationship with you (or because of discussions you had with such attorney). Indeed, bringing a new lawyer or law firm into the case may cause your employer (and you) unwanted delay and additional costs. That may – or may not – enhance your bargaining position.

On the other hand, where the process is not going to be acrimonious, and you are senior enough to play a role in the selection or regular use of outside corporate counsel, an informal referral from the company's counsel may be fine. In any event, you should not discuss your views, thought processes, theories or claims with your employer's counsel – his job is to aggressively represent the interests of your employer without regard to his personal feelings about you.

5.3. How Do I Find The Right Lawyer?

There are a variety of sources that you can access in order to research the names of competent employment counsel. Among sources that individuals have found to be valuable in identifying counsel are the following:

- ▶ Referrals from colleagues or other employees who recently have been through this process

- ▶ Referrals from your accountant or tax adviser

- ▶ Referrals from your family's general practice lawyer

- ▶ Cold calls to senior partners in labor law firms which exclusively represent management asking for a recommendation of a good plaintiff's lawyer

- ▶ Referral from a local or state bar association

- ▶ Lawyers who have authored articles and/or books on the subject of employment law or terminations

- ▶ Directories of lawyers

▶   On-line search vehicles and web-sites

The internet continues to grow as a rich source of virtually any type of information you want: attorneys with specific areas of expertise, in specific states or cities, who have litigated cases involving your specific issue, etc. While the internet has made such searches easier in some respect, you can also get overwhelmed with information. Remember, that much of what you access on the internet is paid advertising by lawyers rather than objective information.

The lawyer with whom you consult should be able to fully evaluate the facts and circumstances surrounding your employment relationship with your employer and the events specifically leading up to the termination of your employment. A knowledgeable lawyer should be able to provide you with a preliminary evaluation of your legal rights after spending no more than several hours with you.

You should not hesitate to consult with more than one lawyer if you are not sure what to do. It's like getting a second opinion before undergoing open heart surgery. And a second opinion may be appropriate even if you like the lawyer with whom you have met and like what he has to say.

As a general rule: when in doubt, get another view.

5.4.   How Do I Recognize The "Wrong" Lawyer For Me?

You should not gravitate toward the 'big' name attorney just because he is a 'big' name. Most important is your comfort level that the lawyer you engage understands your case and issues; is well versed in applicable areas of law; has experience handling your type of issues; may have prior experience dealing with your employer (although that can sometimes be a negative) and is someone with whom you feel comfortable working. You also want someone who has the time to give you the personal attention that you want (and are willing to pay for).

If you feel that the lawyer talks down to you, he probably is the wrong lawyer for you. If you feel that he is distracted with phone calls or e-mails during your meeting, he probably is the wrong lawyer for you. If the lawyer does not have a good grasp of your facts and issues, he probably is the wrong lawyer for you. And if you had to wait a long time to get an appointment with him or have trouble getting your telephone calls returned in a timely manner, he probably is the wrong lawyer for you.

5.5. What To Expect From The Consultation

Once you have selected the attorney with whom you are going to consult, you should bring all of the documents and information outlined above (Chapter 3) to the initial meeting with the lawyer. You should prepare for the meeting as you would prepare for any business meeting. If your job does not entail these types of regular business meetings, don't despair. Prepare a checklist for yourself before the meeting: make sure that you have all of the relevant documents assembled and organized. Jot down all of the relevant information you want to give to the lawyer and the questions that you want to ask. If you rely upon your memory to cover everything, you are likely to leave things out. Even – or especially – seasoned executives make notes for themselves.

At the consultation, you should be able to clearly articulate why you have sought legal counsel (*i.e.* what information or answers do you want to leave the meeting with). Are you consulting with the lawyer solely to review a separation agreement given to you by your employer? Or are you doing so in order to get advice and determine what, if any, legal rights you have. And you should be prepared, in no more than an hour, to describe yourself, your educational background, your work history, performance evaluations and achievements, and your compensation progressions including your most recent compensation package. Use your notes.

Finally, you should be ready to succinctly describe the facts and circumstances surrounding, and leading up to your separation. Be ready to conclude your presentation with your best guess as to "why" it happened. This is not the time to worry about what you can prove – or even whether you are right. It is useful to give the lawyer some roadmap to pursue based upon your experiences with, and knowledge of your employer and the inside players that counsel can evaluate based upon his expertise in the law. Certainly, in the initial meeting with the attorney, you are in the best position to "guess" as to why your employer took the action it did that landed you in the lawyer's office – you may not be right, and you may not be able to prove it, but that's alright. It's a place to start.

Unless and until you start litigation and the process enters the discovery phase (which means that you have not settled your situation with your employer and have decided to take the matter to court), neither you nor your lawyer has the *right* to insist upon answers to questions or to obtain access to documents or other information from your employer. Those rights exist in litigation, but generally not before. As a result, the fact that your lawyer may not be able to fully evaluate the merits of your situation, let alone the strengths or weaknesses of your position and your employer's counter-position should not be viewed as a deficiency.

You should not expect the initial session with the lawyer to provide you with the definitive answer as to your legal rights. It can't. In fact, even if you decide to hire a lawyer, you are likely to hear the lawyer say "I think", or "it looks/sounds like" or "there is a strong suggestion that . . ." "That is not because the lawyer missed the course on contract law or the one on employment discrimination law. Instead, and unless you have a veritable smoking gun – the definitive document that irrefutably establishes that your legal rights have been violated – the best the lawyer can do at this juncture is to evaluate what you have told and shown to him – *your version of the "facts".*

Also note that as fair and objective as you think your view of what happened may be, rest assured that your employer may have another view. And that's what creates disputes, litigation and settlements. You should expect that there probably will be different interpretations as to matters that you are certain are "fact" or "objectively true". That is even more true when it comes to perceptions of such matters as performance, attitude, whether you "play well with others", attainable business goals, personality and the like.

5.6. How Much Detail Should I Expect (Want) From The Lawyer?

While you should not expect the lawyer to make a legal scholar out of you during the initial meeting, you should be given a basic overview of the general legal rules applicable to your situation. This does not assume litigation; rather it is the predicate for you to be a meaningful participant in evaluating the strength of your legal position and how to leverage it strategically.

This may sound somewhat more complicated than it really is. For example, if your presentation to the lawyer suggests that you may have been the victim of age discrimination, the lawyer should tell you which laws may apply to your case; what age ranges fall within the protection of each such law; and what you would need to prove in order to "win" (*i.e.* proof of your protected status; evidence that you have suffered some legally recognized adverse employment action such as being terminated; and, most important, evidence that there is a nexus, connection, or a demonstrable link between your status and the adverse employment action).

The lawyer should provide the same type of analysis for each of the different potential legal claims that may be suggested by your facts. In most instances, there are a limited number of available legal theories that might apply to your circumstances. As a result, the lawyer should be able to provide you with an overview of the basic legal parameters of each potential claim relatively briefly. Of course, it is possible that your lawyer may identify additional legal claims or theories later, after you have retained him and he becomes fully engaged in your case. He may also reject claims later that he thought might be preliminarily viable.

Armed with a preliminary analysis of your legal position and rights and a sketchy, but somewhat ballpark sense of what those claims might be worth if you were a successful litigant, you should have a candid and specific discussion with the attorney as to approach, strategy, likelihood of success, and legal fees.

5.7. *What If I Have No Case?*

By the end of the initial consultation session with the lawyer, you should be able to walk away with several key pieces of important information. Principally, you should have a strong indication whether the lawyer thinks that you have any legal basis for complaining about your treatment by your employer. If, after all said and done, you are advised that you do not have any viable legal claims, it's time to move on. As hard as it may be to accept, not everybody who has been "screwed" by their employer has a viable legal claim. That does not mean that you should fold your tent and walk away from pursuing negotiations with your employer over separation terms. Rather, it means that you should proceed down the negotiating path somewhat more gingerly and judiciously than if you had a strong legal case.

5.8. *What If My Rights May Have Been Violated?*

If the lawyer's preliminary view is that one or more of your legal rights may have been violated, you should proceed to the next step. You and the lawyer should then explore the various types of legal claims suggested by your facts. For each theory, your lawyer should provide you with enough analysis so that you have an understanding of the basic threshold standards that the law will require in order for a case to be successfully drafted and then prosecuted. At this stage of the process, you still know far more about the facts and circumstances than the lawyer.

If litigation is a viable option for you in the event that negotiations are not successful in reaching a settlement, you and your lawyer should also preliminarily discuss various litigation options and strategies. While the initial meeting with the lawyer is not the time for a comprehensive litigation analysis, it is possible that the strength of your pre-litigation negotiating position may be driven, at least in part, by knowledge of basic litigation strategy. Thus, it may be useful to know the scope of discovery that will be available to you from your employer if a negotiated settlement cannot be achieved and litigation ensues. You may also be dissuaded from litigation because of the cost or because you are not prepared to endure the rigors, time involved and risk of litigation.

Your lawyer should also discuss with you the type and amount of damages that may be available to you with respect to each potential claim that he has identified, and identify the various courts and government agencies with which you can file a lawsuit or claim. The lawyer should also advise you of the relevant time periods or statutes of limitations within which you must file a legal claim. Some such time periods are quite short and you don't want to inadvertently miss a filing deadline.

6.

Third Step Continued – Establishing A Fee Arrangement With Your Lawyer

A key consideration in selecting a lawyer to hire is the cost involved. Now, more than ever before, lawyering is run more like a business. In most law firms, revenue and income are derived solely from the fees earned for professional services provided. Legal fees should be discussed with the lawyer during the initial consultation so that there is no dispute over unmet expectations later on. Once a fee arrangement is agreed upon between you and the lawyer (which may not happen during the initial consultation), the terms of your engagement of the lawyer, including the scope of representation and a description of the legal fees, should be put in writing and signed by you and the lawyer. The retainer agreement or letter of engagement between you and the lawyer or his firm is a contract and it should be easy to understand, free from ambiguity and specify what you and the lawyer can expect from the other.

There are several common fee options that you should discuss with the lawyer. Then take some time to decide which option fits best with your overall situation. Some lawyers and law firms have established fee schedules and will not deviate from them. Others may be flexible in structuring a fee arrangement with you. You can safely assume that if the lawyer thinks that you have a low likelihood of success in your case (and he therefore is assuming greater risk of not getting compensated for his time), he will be less willing to commit to an open ended engagement on a contingent fee basis.

6.1. *Hourly Fee Arrangement*

Under an hourly fee option, you compensate the attorney on a straight hourly fee basis. Here, you will pay for each hour (and fractional hours) which the attorney devotes to your case. There may also be hourly fees charged to you for more junior attorneys who work for your lawyer or his law firm, and maybe fees for paralegals and others who assist your lead counsel. This may be appropriate where research and other matters do not require the personal attention of the lawyer with the highest hourly billing rate and can efficiently be accomplished by junior, less costly attorneys or others.

The straight hourly fee arrangement relieves the lawyer of risk in the event that he is not successful on your behalf and places the entire financial burden for prosecution of your matter on you. The fact that the lawyer is not at financial risk is only part of the story. It also is true that lawyers cannot continue to attract hourly paying clients if they do not deliver results. Some law firms only undertake representation of a client on an hourly basis as a matter of policy. If that is the law firm's policy, you really cannot fairly draw any inference as to the lawyer's view of the strength of your case. If straight hourly billing is the only fee arrangement that the lawyer or his firm offers, and you either cannot afford to pay hourly fees or want your lawyer to have some 'skin in the game', you should consult with other lawyers who are more accommodating of flexible fee arrangements.

If you proceed on an hourly fee basis, you should have a discussion as to which lawyer in the firm will perform each specific function. You undoubtedly want the lead lawyer to be the one to interface with your employer or its lawyer. But, where you opt for an hourly fee arrangement, consideration should be given to whether a junior attorney with your lawyer's firm can efficiently handle certain aspects of the case (with or without supervision by a more senior attorney).

But pay attention to the details: it makes no sense to have a junior attorney spend 2 hours of research time at an hourly billing rate of $250.00 if the lead lawyer can do the same project in 1 hour, albeit at $400.00 per hour. This also goes to the matter of hiring a lawyer with specific employment law expertise. Except where there are novel issues of law, your lawyer should not need to spend time researching (or having others research) basic employment law issues.

You are entitled to a detailed description of the hours devoted by each attorney and the services provided, but you may have to ask for such information if it is not the law firm's standard practice to provide this kind of detail as a matter of course along with its bills. The letter of engagement should specifically address this issue.

The range of hourly rates vary widely depending upon geography (where the lawyer is located), size of firm, firm overhead, name, reputation, expertise of the lawyer and complexity of the representation. If you engage the lawyer on an hourly fee basis, you should expect that the law firm will request that you pay it an initial retainer fee which is up-front money against which the lawyers' time will be charged. To the extent that the actual hours devoted to your matter exceed the amount of the retainer fee, you should expect to be billed for such excess amounts on a monthly, quarterly or other agreed upon basis. If your matter concludes before the retainer fee is exhausted, you should expect that the unused portion of the retainer fee will be returned to you. The fee agreement should address each of these contingencies.

Some lawyers structure their fees in order to stay financially ahead of their client. In such cases, you may be required to continue to replenish the initial retainer you paid the lawyer when the amount remaining after billing falls to a defined level. In that way, there is always 'money in the bank' so that the lawyer is ahead of your billing and not waiting to get paid.

There are several situations where an hourly fee arrangement works well, assuming that you can afford to pay hourly legal fees. One such circumstance is where the expected amount of time required to complete your representation is quite limited. Another is where you anticipate (or hope) that the value added by the lawyer will substantially exceed the cost of his services. For example, if you expect that your lawyer will successfully obtain an increase in the amount of severance offered by your employer from $25,000 to $100,000 at a cost of $10,000 in hourly fees, the hourly fee arrangement might make good sense. Under such circumstances, your cost would be significantly less than if the law firm took the case on a contingent fee arrangement. Of course, the risk is that your expectations of success are unmet and you incur significant hourly fees that do not produce the result you sought or expected.

Some clients are sometimes quite needy and want to talk with their lawyer on a regular (or more frequent) basis. From the lawyer's perspective, that is not an issue if he is being compensated on an hourly basis – make all the calls that you want, but remember that the fee clock is ticking every time your lawyer picks up the phone to speak with you or answers an e-mail from you.

6.2. Straight Contingent Fee Arrangement

A second option involves a purely contingent fee arrangement. Some lawyers like this option because of the financial incentive it provides (*i.e.* the better the result, the more the lawyer is paid). Some clients prefer this option because you are not billed on an hourly time basis and you generally are not required to pay an up-front retainer fee to the firm. Unlike the straight hourly fee arrangement that places the risk on you, the contingent fee arrangement shifts the risk to the law firm. Thus, under the hourly fee arrangement, the firm is compensated for the time it devotes to your representation regardless of the outcome; the lawyer does not get a premium for an outstanding result, but is fully compensated for his time.

However, under a contingent fee arrangement, the lawyer receives no compensation unless there is a pool of money at the end of the representation from which to get paid. Here, the risk is the firm's: if the lawyer is unsuccessful, he gets nothing for the time he devoted to your case. Moreover, even if successful, the lawyer may not be fully compensated for all of the time spent on your case if the contingent fee ends up being less than he would have been paid on a straight hourly basis. Or where the lawyer obtains a great result, but the company is so financially strapped that getting paid is difficult.

Note that it is also true that the lawyer's responsiveness to the "needy" client may be somewhat tempered when he is not be compensated for every call by the client – including those "just checking in" calls. As it turns out, clients who do not pay for the time that they take out of a lawyer's day feel freer to take advantage of this opportunity. Lawyers, being only human, sometimes respond accordingly.

As a result, you should expect that if the lawyer agrees to represent you on a contingent fee basis, the firm will want a significant percentage of the amount it obtains for you as its fee. The contingent fee percentage that you will pay the lawyer can vary and should be negotiated with the attorney – in advance and specified in the fee agreement. As the dollar amounts at issue in negotiations with your employer increase, a sliding scale contingent fee arrangement may be appropriate so that the percentage that you are obligated to pay to the lawyer changes as the amount obtained reaches various, pre-agreed upon thresholds (*i.e.* the lawyer is paid 33 1/3 % of the first defined amount obtained by him; plus 25% of the next defined amount, and so on).

There are a variety of formulas that can be negotiated to establish the lawyer's contingent fee entitlement including an upfront flat retainer plus a reduced contingency percentage or with a credit for the upfront retainer against a contingent fee amount. You should not hesitate to negotiate a fee structure with which you are comfortable, but be sure that the arrangement is fully and clearly explained in the fee agreement.

6.3. Blended Hourly and Contingent Fee Arrangement

A third fee option is a blend of the first two: (A) payment by you of hourly fees that are computed either at a reduced hourly rate or up to a capped, maximum amount; plus (B) a reduced contingent fee under which the percentage is reduced to reflect the shared risk. This approach reduces or limits your outside exposure to legal fees in the event of an unsuccessful result but still provides the lawyer with an upside potential for work well done.

Example:

> The lawyer normally charges $400 per hour for his services. Instead of paying the lawyer at $400 per hour for all of the time that he spends on your case, consider reducing his hourly fee to $200 and adding the payment of a reduced contingent fee such as 15% or 20% to the hourly fees.
>
> By way of example, assume that the lawyer obtained an additional $75,000 of severance for you and spent 25 hours of his time doing so.
>
> If you had a purely contingent fee arrangement with the lawyer, you would pay the lawyer $25,000 (1/3 of the $75,000).
>
> If you had a straight hourly fee arrangement with the lawyer, you would pay the

lawyer $10,000 for the same 25 hours of work at his standard $400 hourly rate.

Now consider a combined hourly/contingent arrangement under which you pay the lawyer ½ of his regular hourly rate plus 15% of the amount obtained. That means that the hourly portion of your fee would be $5,000 ($200/hour x 25 hours) plus $11,250 (15% of $75,000) resulting in a total fee payable by you in the amount of $16,250.

The alternatives present starkly different fee outcomes. Of course, deciding which option to try to negotiate with the lawyer would be much easier if you knew, in advance, the outcome of the lawyer's efforts. But, that's not the way it works.

Whenever a contingent fee is adopted (as the entire fee or as part of blended fee arrangement), it is important to be clear as to the basis upon which the contingent fee percentage will be computed. Generally, you should not be required to pay any fee on the severance or other consideration that was already offered to you by your employer before you retained counsel. Counsel does not have to work for this consideration and, despite the risk that it could be withdrawn, fairness should dictate that all such consideration be excluded from the contingent fee computation.

In addition, where the fee arrangement includes a retainer and/or hourly fee component along with some contingent fee component, you should discuss with your lawyer how any retainer fee and/or hourly fees that you are obligated to pay to the law firm will be handled when computing the contingent fee. Will your employer's initial offer be deducted from the final settlement package before computing the contingent fee? Will the retainer and hourly fees paid by you be credited against the contingent fee (Example A below)? Will the fees paid be deducted "above the line" (Example B below) or "below the line" (Example C below) before the contingent fee percentage is applied? If you are not careful, you may pay legal fees twice on the same package dollar.

There are a number of different ways to structure the fee agreement and they do not all end up in the same place. Indeed, different fee structures can end up costing you significantly different amounts in legal fees.

Let's look at some examples of how the same numbers can result in different bottom lines. As is evident from these examples, there is a significant difference in the amount of legal fees that you might pay based upon the same set of facts – but different fee computation formulas. Take the time to do the calculations so you can negotiate the most favorable deal with your lawyer.

Examples Of The Impact of Various Fee Arrangements

Assume the following:

> Your employer offered you the equivalent of $25,000 in severance and benefits before you hired a lawyer; and

You hired a lawyer and paid him a $5,000 retainer fee (or $5,000 in hourly fees during the course of his representation); and

You agreed to pay the lawyer 25% of the amount obtained by the lawyer that is above the amount of your employer's initial severance offer to you before the lawyer got involved; and

The lawyer negotiates a $75,000 increase in the value of the separation package from the original $25,000 to $100,000.

Example A

One way that your legal fee could be computed is as follows:

	$100,000	Final separation package value
Less	$ 25,000	Amount you were offered before the lawyer got involved
	$ 75,000	Net Recovery upon which 25% contingent fee computed
x	25%	
	$18,750	Gross contingent fee payable by you
Less	$ 5,000	If you are entitled to a credit for retainer and/or hourly fees paid by you
	$ 13,750	Which results in this net contingent fee payable by you

Under this example, you will pay a total fee of $18,750 ($5,000 retainer plus the $13,750 contingency fee). As a result, the $18,750 total amount paid by you computes to a total fee of 25% of the $75,000 additional severance the lawyer obtained for you.

Example B

Same assumptions, but your legal fee agreement is somewhat different and, as a result, your total legal fees would be as follows:

	$100,000	Final separation package value
Less	$ 5,000	First, deduct the retainer and/or hourly fees paid by you
Less	$ 25,000	Then deduct the amount that you were offered before the lawyer got involved
	$ 70,000	Compute the 25% contingent fee on the balance
x	25%	
	$ 17,250	Contingent fee payable by you

Here, you will pay a total legal fee of $22,250 ($5,000 retainer plus the $17,250 contingency fee). As a result, the $22,250 fee ends up being 30% of the $75,000 additional severance the lawyer obtained for you – 5% more than you would have paid under Example A.

Example C

Same assumptions, but consider yet another way of computing your legal fee as follows:

	$100,000	Final separation package value
x	25%	First, compute the contingent fee percentage
	$ 25,000	That gives you the gross legal fee
Less $	5,000	Then, take a credit for retainer or hourly fees paid by you
	$ 20,000	This is your net contingent legal fee

Here, you will pay a total fee of $ 25,000 ($5,000 retainer plus the $20,000 contingent fee) which is 33 1/3% of the additional $75,000 in severance obtained by the lawyer rather than the 25% in Example A.

• • •

As the above examples clearly indicate, there can be a wide spread in total legal fees that are payable based upon the same set of settlement factors, but with varying formulas for the computation of fees. You should spend some time to evaluate the approach that will maximize the net amount you will receive.

6.4. *Flat Fee*

You should also consider a flat fee arrangement with the lawyer. Under this type of arrangement, you generally pay your lawyer an up-front, agreed upon fixed amount which represents the entire fee to which the lawyer is entitled regardless of the outcome of his representation. This arrangement is the least common. That is because the lawyer generally will set a flat fee amount that is high enough to compensate for his efforts in significantly increasing the compensation offered to you while foregoing the potential upside of a larger fee that he might be paid in a contingent fee arrangement. The lawyer also needs to be sure he is compensated in the event that he spends many more hours on your matter than he anticipated.

Clients are almost universally confident that their employer will open the floodgate of cash as soon as it receives a letter from a lawyer. If only that were true. The risk to you of paying a flat fee is that you may well invest a substantial amount of money and end up with less than a stellar result (*i.e.* the investment in fees turned out to be disproportionately large to the outcome).

6.5. *Reducing The Fee Agreement To Writing*

Whether you have agreed upon a straight hourly fee, flat fee, contingent fee or other blended fee arrangement with your lawyer, all of the particulars of the arrangement should be described in a retainer agreement or letter of engagement between you and the lawyer. All such agreements should specify the scope of legal services to be provided by the lawyer, whether other lawyers or staff will be involved and, if so, who will do what on your behalf. They also should specify the event or date on which the lawyer's representation begins and ends.

6.5.1. *What To Include In An Hourly Fee Arrangement*

In the case of an hourly fee arrangement, the engagement letter should specify (i) the hourly rate for each category of individual who may work on your case (*i.e.* partner, senior associate, junior associate, paralegal, legal assistant, clerical staff); (ii) how often you will be billed and how much time you will have to pay each bill; (iii) how long the initial hourly rates will remain in effect until they are subject to change (usually at least 1 year); (iv) how much of an up-front retainer you will required to pay and whether any unused portion will be refunded to you; (v) whether you will be required to replenish the retainer each time the amount of the retainer falls below a certain threshold; and (vi) whether there will be a 'cap' (maximum amount) on the amount of fees for which you will be responsible.

Example 1

> As agreed, our fees in connection with this firm's representation of you will be computed on an hourly fee basis. Specifically, you will be billed by this firm for services rendered at the hourly billing rates of

(i) _____ Dollars ($000.00) per partner and counsel hour (ii) _____ Dollars ($000.00) per associate/counsel and (iii) _____ Dollars ($00.00) per paralegal/legal assistant hour devoted to said representation (all at a pro rata portion thereof for a proportionate amount of time). Hourly fees will be billed against an initial retainer in the amount of _____ Dollars ($0,000.00) payable by you upon execution of this letter agreement. All hourly fees set forth above will remain fixed for a minimum of one (1) year from the date hereof and thereafter are subject to upward adjustment to this firm's then prevailing hourly rates following written notice to you of such changes.

In the event that the amount of time devoted by this firm on your behalf exceeds the time represented by the retainer, you will be billed for any such excess on a periodic basis. In the event there are unearned fees on deposit with this firm upon conclusion of our representation of you, the unearned amount will be refunded to you.

All fees are exclusive of any disbursements which are incurred by this firm in connection with our representation of you which likewise will be billed to you on a periodic, but not more frequent than monthly basis. You agree to pay each and all such bills within thirty (30) days after presentation. All fees are exclusive of any disbursements which are incurred by our firm in connection with our representation which likewise will be billed to you on a periodic, but not more frequent than monthly basis.

Example 2

You may be asked to deposit one or more additional retainers with this firm to be billed against professional legal fees if, as and when the amount of professional fees due to this firm are expected to exhaust the amount of the retainer then on deposit.

6.5.2. What To Include In A Contingent Fee Arrangement

Where the fee agreement contains a contingent fee component, you should expect that the fee agreement will be more detailed. In addition to a description of how the contingent fee will be computed (*see* above examples), the engagement letter should carefully detail each of the various components of the separation package upon which the contingent fee will be computed. This is not as easy as it sounds and careful attention to these details is important.

▶ *How To Handle Cash or Cash Equivalents*

Some elements of the severance package are readily identifiable and easy to compute. Cash, as in severance pay and salary continuation, is one such example. Payment by your employer of your COBRA or other insurance premiums, contributions to deferred compensation, country club dues and fees, 401(k) and other such type plans are others.

▶ *How To Handle Equity (Stock & Options)*

Then there are less easily quantified components. Stock and other types of equity grants that become immediately vested and exercisable can be valued according to generally accepted valuation methodology. But what happens if you decide not to sell the stock? Are you obligated to pay a legal fee on the value of the benefit obtained by counsel even though the cash is still tied up in the stock itself? If so, as of what date?

How about stock options and other types of equity programs that may, but do not necessarily, have a future value? What will be the methodology for valuing these benefits for purposes of computing the attorney's fee?

▶ *How To Handle Other Non-Cash Benefits*

Non-cash benefits such as outplacement services, use of an office and secretarial assistance for a defined period of time, company paid executive medical or physical examinations, company paid tax advice and/or financial planning, continued use or the below market sale or transfer to you of a company owned/lease automobile or computer, agreement by your employer not to contest unemployment insurance benefits, etc. present the greatest challenge.

If your lawyer expects to be paid for the value of these benefits, you should include a specific valuation methodology in the engagement agreement. While some of these benefits may be susceptible to easy valuation (and some may not), the better approach may be to exclude such items from the value of the separation package upon which legal fees are computed. By doing so, you avoid disputes with your lawyer as to proper valuation as well as the cost of valuation.

In addition, you should be cautious about agreeing to pay a fee on non-cash benefits that do not generate immediate settlement cash to you from which you can write the fee check. By way of example, are you obligated to pay a fee on additional monthly retirement benefits that resulted from negotiations to add years of credited service or years added to your age? Will you pay the increased benefit amount to the lawyer each month? Will you value the increased benefit based upon actuarial assumptions as to potential future value even though they may not generate any immediate cash? How will you value retiree medical benefits to which you become entitled years from now as a result of negotiations with your employer?

Let's assume by way of another example that the actuarial value of a post-retirement health benefit for the balance of your life that was negotiated by your lawyer is $200,000 (assuming that you live long enough to enjoy the full value of this benefit). If your fee agreement obligates you to pay your lawyer a 25% contingency fee ($50,000) on that amount, you may find yourself in a difficult financial bind. And what happens if you die before you ever start using the benefit?

Moreover, the value of one or more of these benefits may become apparent only in the middle of negotiations which may be the worst time for the issue to rear its head.

Consider your proposal that your employer pay your club dues for an additional year as the final sweetener just to close the deal. This concept had not come up previously nor was it specifically addressed in the engagement letter. You and your lawyer may feel very differently about whether the amount of the dues being paid by the company on your behalf should be included when computing the contingent fee if the club dues are $50,000 a year rather than $2,500.

If the rest of the separation package provides your lawyer with the potential for handsome compensation, charging you for some of these peripheral benefits may make the attorney appear chintzy – although that won't necessarily stop him from trying to collect. Care must be exercised in defining the elements of the package that will be valued and included when computing the fee to be paid to your lawyer.

Examples:

You agree to pay this firm ___% of the Gross Recovery which means and includes the gross, pre-tax value of all consideration of any kind paid or to be paid to you or received or to be received by you (whether by lump sum pay-out, salary continuance, structured payments over time or otherwise) as well as the cash value of all other component parts of such settlement including, but not limited to, funds contributed by Employer toward any pension, retirement, 401K or other deferred plan, all types of insurance and any and all other fringe benefits, value of vesting of unvested stock, options, grants or awards, additional service or age years of credit for retirement benefit purposes (using a recognized valuation method such as Black-Scholes).

and

The Gross Recovery will be reduced by (i) the amount of the retainer fee selected and paid by you; and (ii) the consideration set forth in the Separation Agreement and General Release to you from Employer dated _____, and the percentage contingent legal fee due to this firm will be computed on the balance.

Or

The percentage contingent legal fee due to this firm will be computed on the Gross Recovery and that amount will then be reduced by (i) the amount of the retainer fee selected and paid by you above; and (ii) the consideration set forth in the Separation Agreement and General Release to you from Employer dated _____.

6.5.3. *Taking Tax Considerations Into Account*

The factor that may have the greatest financial impact in valuing the package upon which your legal fees will be computed is whether to use the gross, pre-tax value of the package, or some other amount which is intended to take your income tax liability into account. Given the changing nature of the tax laws, you should preliminarily determine whether legal fees paid by you to your lawyer will be deductible by you from your income taxes and, if so, the extent of the deduction to which you will be entitled and the cash value of any such deduction.

If your legal fees are deductible, the actual, after-tax cost of those fees will be reduced by the tax savings you experience as a result of the deduction. However, if the legal fees are non-deductible, in whole or in part, that means that out of every dollar you receive in the separation package (especially where the package includes valuations for non-cash assets), you will have to pay both your lawyer and the government (although not necessarily in that order). You are left with the balance. Situations where a lawyer receives a larger share of a separation package than the net amount received by a client are not unheard of, and should be avoided.

If your fee agreement contemplates taking taxes into consideration, be sure to define which taxes are relevant. It also is important to specify when the legal fees are to be paid to your lawyer. It may make a difference if your tax returns will not be prepared for many months after the settlement closes. In such event, you may not know your true tax position until then.

For example, will carry-forward and other current losses, capital gains/losses (including on any equity portion of the separation agreement) change your tax bracket and thereby impact the base amount upon which the contingent fee percentage is computed? And, of course, with respect to those benefits that do not accrue or vest for years to come, or stock options that currently are 'under water' or that you do not exercise for years, it is virtually impossible to accurately assess the tax burden for those out-years. Will your lawyer wait to be paid until all such calculations have been made? Unlikely. Will he have the right to review your tax returns? That should be avoided. Will he have the right to object to the way the tax returns are prepared? That should also be avoided.

Use of the after tax value of the package to compute fees also means that the amount you owe the lawyer in legal fees might vary depending upon the year in which the settlement is made. It also means that the lawyer may receive widely disparate compensation from 2 different clients who receive identical settlements but have very different tax positions.

Thus, and unless there is a compelling reason to use an after tax valuation, you should strongly consider computing legal fees on the gross settlement amount. The gross number obviously will be larger, but you can mitigate the tax implications by carefully defining the amount upon which attorney's fees will be computed (*i.e.* the contingent fee percentage computed on 75% of the gross settlement amount instead of the entire amount; or either by reducing the contingency percentage and/or excluding certain benefits from fee computation).

6.5.4. Defining When Legal Fees Are Payable

The fee agreement should also address the timing of when you are obligated to pay your legal fees. Are you obligated to pay the legal fees upon execution of the separation agreement with the employer even though you may receive cash and other benefits over time or at some point in the future? Do you pay the fees only if, as and when the cash and other benefits are actually received by you? That might mean that you and the law firm could be partners for years to come – especially if you are going to use an after-tax valuation method. What happens if your employer does not make all of the severance or salary continuation payments that the separation agreement calls for? Are you entitled to a refund from the lawyer for fees paid by you on the portion of the settlement that your employer never paid to you?

6.5.5. What About Disbursements And Expenses?

Most fee agreements require that you pay for disbursements or expenses incurred by the attorney. You should be sure that you understand the types and amounts of charges for which you will be billed so that you are not surprised later. Per page facsimile transmittals, photocopying, postage, meals, travel (airfare, hotel, car rental, etc.), conference room usage, telephone, conference and long distance calls, on-line subscription search services, investigators (outside and law firm employees), hand deliveries and overnight mail are a few. Some lawyers charge a flat percentage of their legal fee to cover all such disbursements and expenses. While this saves a lot of bookkeeping for the lawyer, it also can be a significant additional amount that you have to pay. Some expenses can add substantially to your bill and you should consider requiring the lawyer to obtain your prior approval before his expenditure of these expenses.

Your fee agreement with the lawyer should define whether (a) expenses will be billed to you and payable on an ongoing basis or accumulated until the matter concludes (as is generally done with contingent fee arrangements); (b) your lawyer will be reimbursed first for his expenses and disbursements out of the separation package (thereby reducing the gross package amount) with the contingent legal fee computed on the balance; or (c) the contingent fee is computed on the gross, pre-expense/disbursement amounts of the settlement and the expenses added to that amount increasing the total amount due from you to the lawyer [that reduces your net even more]; or (d) the contingent legal fee includes expenses so that there is no separate charge for expenses. There may be significant differences.

• • •

Once you have an agreed upon a fee arrangement with counsel, a written fee agreement (in letter form or otherwise) should be prepared by the lawyer and signed by you and the lawyer. Be sure to carefully review the agreement to ensure that it accurately details all of the issues discussed above.

7.

"JUICE - I"
Leverage vs. Risk

Successful negotiations flow from the leverage, or perceived leverage, that each party brings to the negotiating table. In fact, the perception that a party has leverage can be as important as actually having it. To begin with, leverage – otherwise referred to as '*JUICE*' – does not exist simply because you want to have it, or because you believe that you're right. Instead, leverage is the product of something that a party brings to negotiations that causes the other party to reassess its position.

There are different sources of leverage. Perhaps you have leverage because your employer knows that it has violated your legal rights. Or because your employer cannot afford the cost of litigation, even if it is confident of victory and vindication. Or because your employer needs, or wants to keep the matter private and is unwilling to have the dispute aired in public. Or because your employer (or individual members of management) cannot risk having unfavorable or potential damaging or problematic information aired in litigation. Or because management wants to avoid adverse publicity. Or because your employer . . . .

But leverage usually is not a one way street. Your employer may have leverage of its own. Perhaps you engaged in conduct that you cannot afford to have aired in public, especially while you are looking for a new job. Or you were accused of misconduct resulting in an inconclusive investigation, but with a cloud remaining over your head. Or because the company's lawyers have advised management that you have no legal case. Or because your employer does not believe that you are willing to go to the mat and sue. Or because your employer is holding a positive job reference for you hostage. Or because you already confided in someone (who disloyally has told management) what you really want and how far you are willing to go. Or because you . . . .

A caveat to the foregoing is appropriate. Your analysis of whether you have leverage, the type of leverage you think you have, and how much *JUICE* the leverage will give you, rests upon the flawed assumption that both you and your employer will act rationally. That is a risky bet. Even if both you and your employer accurately, and similarly, assess your leverage, it may still be irrelevant.

Sometimes an employer just doesn't care what you do and, against all advice, has decided not to give in and settle with you. That could happen even when you should have lots of *JUICE*, but your employer is intent on dragging you down with it. Or where your employer wants to send a message about the risk of tangling with the company to other employees who might consider challenging the company in the future.

Common sense also dictates that the more aggressive you get (and the more personal the claims you assert), the greater the risk that your employer's original offer may be withdrawn. Thus, logic, rational analysis and assumptions about the exercise of sound business judgment sometimes gets you nowhere when you are trying to evaluate your *JUICE*. That's because sometimes it's not always about logic, rational analysis or sound business judgment – instead, it may be about anger, emotional hostility or outright vindictiveness.

When dealing with an employer that is ready to throw sound business judgment to the wind, even the most well conceived personal business plan that relies upon the most reasonable assessment of *JUICE*, likely will fail. The key, underlying assumption about how reasonable businesses act becomes inoperative to your employer.

The problem is compounded when you and your employer evaluate the strength of your *JUICE* differently, even when looking at the same set of facts. Perhaps one of you has been given very different legal advice than the other and view the downside risk of possible litigation differently. That can happen even when everyone is acting rationally and in good faith. Law is not strictly black and white. Lawyers evaluating the same set of facts can – and do – reach different conclusions.

However, when dealing with a more rational employer, you should assume that if your assessment of your *JUICE* is reasonably accurate, your employer has – or will – draw essentially the same conclusions, albeit from a different perspective. For example, your employer likely will factor into its own evaluation the applicable taxes and legal fees that are payable by you in calculating the bottom line or the net 'spread' between the package already offered to you and the one now demanded by you.

Despite the pitfalls inherent in assessing your own, and your employer's leverage strengths and pressure points, doing so is a key ingredient in the development of your personal business plan. Deciding how much *JUICE* you think you can bring to the negotiations necessarily starts with an understanding and assessment of the strength of your position – both your legal position and your practical position. It is the crux of your strategic planning.

With respect to *JUICE* that comes from the strength of your legal position: do you have legal rights that should enhance your negotiating position? Do you have a single strong legal claim? Do you have a potential, but weak legal claim? Will your claim be difficult to prove? Figuring out the answers to those questions is one of the primary reasons for consulting with a lawyer.

Obviously, a lawyer will be less able to assess leverage that is derivative of non-legal considerations. While lawyers regularly are involved in matters where they are required to deal with the practical considerations involved in a litigation, transaction or negotiation, you are probably in the best position to identify specific facts that may yield practical leverage. You and your lawyer should evaluate each such consideration and attempt to assess the relative *JUICE* that each may provide.

You should accept that your employer will likely be resistant to paying you in response to a 'non-legal' claim – especially if the claim smacks of extortion. Neither you nor your lawyer should ever enter that realm. However, it is an entirely different matter where an employer makes a business decision to avoid disclosure of matters which inevitably will be aired in connection with a claim that you assert in litigation.

Clients often express confidence that their employer will act in a certain way; or act predictably; or won't do something; or will be afraid of adverse publicity; or will pay anything to avoid litigation. The appropriate lawyerly response is: "If you knew your employer as well as you think you do, you probably would not be sitting here talking to me."

Assuming that you are not consulting a lawyer strictly as an intellectual exercise or for "moral vindication", the real (even if unspoken) reason for finding out whether you have any legal rights is to assess the strength of your legal position. That, in turn, instructs the *JUICE* that you might be able to bring to negotiations. What this really involves is a judgment (guess) as to how much 'punch' any legal rights you may have will carry in negotiations with your employer and how can it be used.

As a general proposition, the stronger the legal claim that you have, the greater your *JUICE*. And, presumably, as the risk to your employer of testing the strength of your claim or testing your resolve to pursue the claim increases, so does your *JUICE*. But remember, business and management do not always act rationally or even view things the way you do. As a result, you may think that you have lots of *JUICE* but end up getting no leverage from it. Great claim, great theory, should be great leverage, but your employer refuses to play!

Once you understand whether you have any legal rights, you can then evaluate how a separation package that has been offered to you stacks up against the potential value of the legal rights you potentially have. If it turns out that you have limited, or no legal rights that your lawyer thinks can be asserted as a result of the termination of your employment, you properly should look at any separation package that is offered to you in a very different light than you would if have valuable legal rights – *BIG JUICE*.

Example:

> Suppose your lawyer advises you that you have no legal rights after reviewing the circumstances surrounding the termination of your employment. Notwithstanding the absence of rights, your employer offers you a separation package worth $100,000. If you are an executive or highly compensated player, you may view that package as wholly inadequate in light of the many years of blood, sweat and profits you have bestowed upon your employer.

Putting aside any moral appeal that argument may hold, however, the $100,000 – by definition – is $100,000 more than you are entitled to in the absence of any legal rights.

Conversely, if you are advised by your attorney that you have legal rights that may be worth between $1MM and $2MM, you can better evaluate the fairness of the $100,00 offer against the potential "full" value gross entitlement of $2MM should you succeed in hitting a "home-run" either in negotiations with your employer or in litigation. Depending upon the actual numbers, the spread between the employer's original offer and the amount of the theoretical "home-run" sometimes makes pursuing the gold ring patently unattractive and illusory – and disproportionately risky.

Thus, an integral part of any personal business plan is your analysis as to whether the net spread between the value of the severance package offered to you by your employer and the upside potential outlined by your lawyer is worth the risk and cost of the chase. While it may not be possible to quantify the risk, you should not ignore the possibility (as contrasted with the probability) that the original package offered by your employer may be withdrawn, either as a matter of corporate policy, or as leverage by the company, or because the time within which to accept it expires, or because a more senior decision maker gets ticked off at your efforts to extract more money from the corporate coffers.

Indeed, the possibility that a package may be withdrawn by your employer may dramatically change your assessment of the spread. As a general rule, most employers do not withdraw separation package offers just because you try to negotiate an enhancement to the package that has been offered. There may even be a basis for a separate legal claim if your employer does so. That likely means that if you decide to pursue negotiations with your employer, the risk that the originally offered package will be withdrawn is 'low' – but not 'no' – risk. And don't look to your lawyer for assurances that the package won't be withdrawn; he does not have a crystal ball and you should factor the possibility of withdrawal into your risk assessment. Even the remote, unlikely possibility that the package will be withdrawn does not mean that it won't be.

The rationale underlying the general assumption that the risk of withdrawal is 'low', but not 'no' risk, is that the original package presumably was offered to you by your employer, at least in part, in order to induce you to sign the separation agreement and the general release from all claims you might have that is in the agreement. In addition, your employer may be trying to secure your agreement to such other conditions as maintaining confidentiality and keeping yourself available for future consultation in the event the need arises. Withdrawal of a package that was originally offered to you would increase the likelihood that you would do exactly the opposite of what the employer was trying to accomplish by offering the package to you in the first place.

In sum, your employer is trying to buy closure of its relationship with you by offering the original package. It wants to eliminate the potential for a contingent liability, possible litigation, and move forward. Withdrawal of an offered package can only increase the likelihood that you will enmesh your employer in just the type of litigation it was seeking to avoid. That's because your downside risk (*i.e.* the risk that the offered package might be withdrawn) has been eliminated. Your employer's offer has been withdrawn and there is therefore no spread left to consider.

While the foregoing is a fair analysis of the 'general rule' of risk, you should remember that you cannot take the 'general rule' to the bank. Remember: 'low', is not 'no' risk. Mostly, this is not a legal analysis; rather it is an assessment of your employer's likely reaction to your efforts to extract additional consideration. You are probably the only one who can even remotely evaluate this risk. You know the players, the company's historical practice and its corporate culture better than your lawyer. In the end, either you are risk averse or you are not. If you are unwilling, or unable to assume any risk (*i.e.* the risk that the offered severance package will be withdrawn), stop here and proceed with finalizing the language in the proposed agreement and leave the money part of the agreement 'as is'.

Without intending to beat the proverbial dead horse, the lawyer's experience here is worth appreciating. Every employment lawyer wishes they had a dollar (at least in 1950 money) for every client who sat across their desk and was absolutely confident that their employer was publicity shy, litigation averse and would pay big money upon receiving a lawyer's demand letter. And almost everyone is convinced that their employer will bend to their will when confronted by a well-known lawyer, or in the face of some claim which raises a "sensitive" issue.

If only that were true. Almost everyone has heard a story from a colleague, co-worker, friend, neighbor, relative or accountant, or has read a newspaper article about a disgruntled ex-employee who pursued his or her employer and got "a lot of money". Maybe the story is accurate; maybe not. Having a potential legal right and deciding what to do with it is no easy task. Indeed, just because you have a legal right (assuming that you do), there is absolutely nothing that requires that you seek vindication of that right.

Some individuals are weakly motivated or even disinclination to pursue even strong legal claims. There also are other individuals who have a strong determination to pursue their employer, even in the face of a weak legal position. The latter are those individuals with strong desire and probably weak *JUICE*; the former may have more *JUICE* but it doesn't matter – they are not terribly interested. Thus, there is a wide range along which you can exercise legitimate judgment as to what to do – if anything.

That said, neither you nor counsel should pursue a claim which is without legal merit or factual basis. Don't make it up. For those claims that fall on the right side of the line – no matter how close – you are free to pursue any permissible course of action. While there is no inherently right answer that dictates what you do, the answer must be right for you. Not for your lawyer and not for your friend, colleague or anyone else.

Thus, consulting with an attorney at the first moment at which it becomes clear that a change in your employment relationship may occur may permit the dynamics of the employment relationship to be redefined or re-positioned through careful strategic planning – creating *JUICE*. It is hard to undo employment actions once they have been announced and implemented.

A cautionary word: except in the most unusual circumstance, it would be imprudent for any employee to introduce an attorney directly into the employment relationship at too early a juncture. Rather, at the early stages before any formal action has been taken by your employer, the attorney is best utilized in a behind-the-scenes role counseling and advising you as circumstances develop.

8.

"JUICE - II"
The Economics Of Risk & Reward

Depending upon how your attorney evaluates the strength of your legal position, the risk/reward calculus should be relatively straightforward. The "spread" (the difference between conceptual "full value" of your legal rights versus the "offer" in the package) becomes the real marker for determining whether the chase for additional compensation is worthwhile. Consider what that really means to you.

Both sides to a negotiation can approximate the net value of a marginal settlement dollar. You may be able to be more precise than your employer in doing so because you have inside information concerning your tax position, but your employer probably can make a pretty good guesstimate. The 2 key variables that reduce a 'gross' settlement dollar are taxes and attorneys' fees.

Over time, the tax laws have changed concerning the taxability of settlement dollars as have tax rates generally. Because Congress and the Internal Revenue Service have an institutional practice of tinkering with the tax laws and rules, you should be sure to consult with competent tax counsel or an accountant who can properly guide you through the current state of law and the tax consequences of a package. In particular, you want to be sure that you are properly guided in terms of the taxability of the various categories of payment in the package which may depend upon how the settlement agreement is drafted and the purpose for which the compensation is being paid to you.

In addition, and likewise depending upon the nature and characterization of the payments, consideration should be given to the issue of the Social Security and Medicare payroll taxes.

Currently, the employee's portion of Social Security (FICA) portion of the tax exceeds 6% of an annually increasing amount of your base compensation up to an annual 'cap' set by Congress from time-to-time. Depending upon the date during the calendar year on which your separation occurs and the amount of your compensation, you may have already paid the year's maximum Social Security tax. As a result, if the severance payments are all made to you during the same calendar year in which your employment terminates and you have reached the annual taxable cap, you will not owe additional Social Security taxes on the package amount (which means that the severance may be worth 6+% more than if it is paid to you in the following year). To the extent severance payments stretch into two or more years (and depending upon your subsequent employment status), you may be required to pay additional Social Security taxes that will reduce your net severance amount.

The Medicare tax (currently almost 1.5%) is less problematic in terms of the timing of severance payments. As currently constituted, the Medicare tax is payable on all eligible compensation paid to you. There is no maximum or annual cap as there is with the Social Security tax. Thus, you will be required to pay the applicable Medicare tax on all severance pay regardless of the year(s) in which it is paid to you, making timing of the severance payments essentially irrelevant, at least with respect to the Medicare tax.

The amount of each settlement dollar that you have agreed to pay your lawyer is the second element. Various fee structures were discussed above in Chapter 5. Part of evaluating whether the upside of potential additional compensation is worth the downside risk and cost to you of the chase is the spread discussed above – the potential net cash bottom line to you, taking into account the tax (federal, state and local) collector's share and your attorney's share. By applying this type of analysis, you can get a pretty good perspective as to whether to assume the risk of the chase.

Examples:

The following examples assume several things:

First, they assume that your attorney has been able to identify one or more viable legal claims which might serve as the basis for a claim in negotiations or in litigation in the event you cannot informally resolve matters with your employer.

Second, the examples assume that your attorney will be compensated on a contingent fee basis and receive either a straight 1/3 contingency fee or a fee representing a total of 1/3 of the net value added (1/3 of the amount received in the settlement that is above the original offer you received from your employer before you retained the attorney to represent you).

Third, the examples assume that the combined federal, state and local taxes (income and payroll) payable by you on the settlement will amount, in the aggregate, to 1/3, after attorneys' fees. The 1/3 tax bite is used for ease of example; it is possible that the actual effective tax impact on you may be significantly different.

Fourth, the examples assume that the original package offered to you by your employer was $250,000. If you had accepted this package as originally offered, you would have netted $166,667 ($250,000 less the assumed 1/3 taxes in the amount of $83,333), because there would be no attorneys' fees payable by you.

Example 1:

> **Original Offer:** $250,000
> **Original Net to You:** $166,667

Now Assume:
- ▶ **You retain counsel to negotiate**
- ▶ **Negotiations increase the original offer (New Settlement Offer column)**
- ▶ **Attorneys' fees are payable by you on straight 1/3 contingent fee basis (fees paid on entire package)**
- ▶ **Taxes are payable on net recovery, after deduction for attorney's fees (Column 'C' computed as 1/3 x 'A' – 'B')**

'A'	'B'	'C'	'D'	'D' - $166,667
New Settlement Offer	1/3 Contingent Fee	Income Taxes	Your Net Recovery	Difference of New Package Over Original
1,000,000	333,333	222,222	444,445	277,778
750,000	250,000	166,667	333,333	166,666
500,000	166,667	111,111	222,222	55,555
400,000	133,333	88,889	177,778	11,111
300,000	100,000	66,667	133,333	(33,334)

Example 2:

Original Offer: $250,000
Original Net to You: $166,667

Now Assume:
- ▶ You retain counsel to negotiate
- ▶ Negotiations increase the original offer (New Settlement Offer column)
- ▶ Attorneys' fees are payable by you on a straight 1/3 contingent fee basis (fees paid on entire package)
- ▶ Taxes are payable on total recovery including attorney's fees paid by you (Column 'C' computed as 1/3 x 'A')

'A'	'B'	'C'	'D'	'D' - $166,667
New Settlement Offer	1/3 Contingent Fee	Income Taxes	Your Net Recovery	Difference of New Package Over Original
1,000,000	333,333	333,333	333,334	166,667
750,000	250,000	250,000	250,000	83,333
500,000	166,666	166,667	166,667	– 0 –
400,000	133,333	133,333	133,334	(33,333)
300,000	100,000	100,000	100,000	(66,667)

Example 3:

        Original Offer: $250,000
        Original Net to You: $166,667

Now Assume:
- ▶ **You retain counsel to negotiate**
- ▶ **Negotiations increase the original offer (New Settlement Offer column)**
- ▶ **Attorneys' fees are payable by you on a 1/3 contingent fee basis computed only on the amount added to package above original $250,000 offer (Column 'B' Computed as 'A' - $250,000 x 1/3)**
- ▶ **Taxes are payable on net recovery after attorney's fees (Column 'C' computed as 1/3 x 'A'–'B')**

'A'   'B'   'C'   'D'   'D' - $166,667
("A" - $250,000)

New Settlement Offer	1/3 Contingent Fee	Income Taxes	Your Net Recovery	Difference of New Package Over Original
1,000,000	250,000	250,000	500,000	333,333
750,000	166,666	194,444	388,890	222,223
500,000	83,333	138,889	277,778	111,111
400,000	50,000	116,666	233,334	66,667
300,000	16,666	94,444	188,890	22,223

Example 4:

        Original Offer: $250,000
        Original Net to You: $166,667

Now Assume:
- **You retain counsel to negotiate**
- **Negotiations increase the original offer (New Settlement Offer column)**
- **Attorneys' fees are payable by you on a 1/3 contingent fee basis only on the amount added to package above the original $250,000 offer**
- **Taxes are payable on total recovery including attorney's fees payable by you (Column 'C' computed as 1/3 x 'A')**

'A'	'B' ("A" - $250,000)	'C'	'D'	'D'-$166,667
New Settlement Offer	1/3 Contingent Fee	Income Taxes	Your Net Recovery	Difference of New Package Over Original
1,000,000	250,000	333,333	416,667	250,000
750,000	166,666	250,000	333,334	166,667
500,000	83,333	166,667	250,000	83,333
400,000	50,000	133,333	216,667	50,000
300,000	16,666	100,000	183,334	16,667

As is evident from Example 1 and based upon the applicable assumptions, the potential changes in the net value to you as a result of the chase becomes stark: if the package is increased by $150,000 (from $250,000 to $400,000), the net value added to you is about $11,000. Even though the separation package has grown by $150,000 – or a 60% increase over the employer's original offer –the value added to you is only marginal. However, if you were able to increase the package by $750,000, or 300% (from $250,000 to $1,000,000), you would add more than $277,000 to your bottom line. But also note that if you added only $50,000 to the package, you might actually end up with substantially less than if you had assumed no risk at all and simply accepted your employer's original offer.

As is evident from Example 2, even where the efforts of your wise and skillful lawyer result in doubling the package offered to you from $250,000 to $500,000, you could be worse off than if you had assumed no risk at all and simply taken the package as originally offered! As a result, you should re-read Chapter 5. Be as careful in negotiating a fee arrangement with your attorney as you are in negotiating your exit package with your employer.

The only change between the scenarios in Examples 1 and 2 is that your tax bill has grown significantly based upon the assumption that you will be taxed on the total recovery, even though your attorney received a big piece of the package. Each person's tax position is different. So are the tax rules that apply depending upon the nature (*e.g.* are you receiving severance, salary continuation, non-cash benefits, payment in settlement of a discrimination claim, damages for emotion distress or other physical injuries that you suffered, etc.) and structure of the payments (when you will be taxed on the consideration being paid to you; payment by your employer of your legal fees directly to your attorney) and the state in which you live. As a result, a critical early part of developing your personal business plan should include consultation with your accountant or tax advisor to determine the net effect of possible scenarios such as the above.

In addition to the change in tax consequences, Examples 3 and 4 assume that attorneys' fees are payable by you only on the value added by your attorney: he is paid only on the increase in amount of the final package over the original offer from your employer before counsel got involved – paying the lawyer for the value added by his lawyering.

The bottom financial line is whether the marginal additional amount of money that is realistically achievable by hiring a lawyer and trying to negotiate additional compensation truly represents the gold ring or is possibly illusory. Doubling the amount of your package sounds like a worthy chase, but, as shown above, the devil is in the details.

The unquantifiable part of this equation, however, is your judgment as to whether your employer will actually increase, double or even quadruple its offer to you, even assuming that you think that the chase is worthwhile. Moreover, remember that while an additional $500,000 obtained through negotiations may only net you an additional $83,333 (see Example 2), it still is an additional $500,000 cost to your employer. Thus, depending upon who is looking at these numbers – and how strongly your attorney has valued your legal rights – the same dollar figure may look very different.

After all is said and done, the decision you reach after consulting with an attorney and studying the issues raised in this Handbook can be reduced to this: *JUICE, JUICE, JUICE* . . . . . how much do you have and what's it worth? That evaluation is based, in large measure, upon the combined factors of how much are you potentially entitled to; how much is being offered; what is the cost of the chase; how willing or averse are you to assume the risk of the chase; the importance of the potential upside of additional compensation to you; and how confident are you in your ability to accurately evaluate the likelihood of success, knowing what you do about the company and the players involved in the decision making process.

Part Two

How Much And What Kind Of Leverage Do You Have?

Part Two of this Handbook addresses the technical aspects of evaluating whether you have *JUICE*. As was discussed in Part One, leverage can result from a limited number of circumstances. The greatest leverage probably comes from identifying that one or more of your legal rights may have been violated by your employer's actions. But even where you do not have a legal claim, you may nevertheless have some degree of leverage due to non-legal, practical considerations that may cause your employer to re-evaluate its position and offer additional compensation.

This Part provides an overview of the types of legal rights that you may have and provides a roadmap for your discussions with a lawyer in order to evaluate whether you have any such rights.

This Part also discusses various types of non-legal factors that should be considered, along with the practical implications that may be relevant to an attempt to leverage such factors in negotiations with your employer.

9.

Termination Of The Employment Relationship

The legal issues surrounding an employment termination invariably are important to formulating a successful strategy. Thus, while this Handbook is not intended to be a resource encyclopedia through the thicket of employment law, you should arm yourself with a basic understanding of the most fundamental concepts of employment law. This will provide you with an analytic framework for your questions and discussions with an attorney who should be able to provide answers to some of your questions. Chapters 9 – 12 will give you a basic snapshot of these rights.

During an initial consultation, a lawyer can only evaluate the legal merits of your situation based upon the facts, information and documents that you provide. As a result, it is incumbent upon you to be sure that you provide the lawyer with as much information as you can, and in as coherent, clear and complete a manner as you can. *See* Chapter 3.

9.1. ***The Employment At-Will Rule***

The baseline legal status of virtually all employment relationships, in all jurisdictions in the United States, is commonly referred to as "at-will". In layman's terms, that means that both you and your employer have the absolute, unfettered, unrestricted, unconditional and unlimited legal right to terminate your employment relationship with the other – with or without cause, justification or reason – and with or without any advanced notice. In sum, the employment relationship in most jurisdictions is moment-to-moment. Either party can bail out, or throw out the other on a whim.

The same generally is true about an employer's right to unilaterally change or eliminate any term, condition or aspect of employment – those too, generally are "at-will". That means that all of the benefits, perquisites and compensation arrangements that you enjoy are subject to change by your employer at any time. Such changes generally must be prospective in nature: your employer cannot change your compensation, benefits and the like today, but make the change effective yesterday – it can only make changes on a going forward basis.

It is often surprising how swift an involuntary termination of employment can happen to an unsuspecting employee. The concept that you can find yourself out of a job at any time, without reason, is simply confounding to most employees. Nevertheless, that's the rule. The theory underlying the at-will employment relationship assumes three things.

First, the at-will rule assumes that both you and your employer have equal rights – each can both jettison the other whenever it/you want. This is technically true. Thus, while the at-will rule permits your employer to decide to terminate your employment on a whim, there also is generally nothing that would preclude you from accepting a new position, relocating to a new city at your new employer's expense, establishing yourself in your new community and then simply never returning to work at your former employer without any notice whatsoever. Or turning up as an executive at your employer's competitor across town.

But this assumed level playing field is really a fiction – especially in tight labor markets and difficult economic times. While a business may not miss a step or two when it terminates the employment of one or more of its employees or one or more employees resign without notice, it is not quite so easy for an employee to successfully leave his employer in the same type of lurch. Interviews, reference checks and the industry grape vine are among the limiting factors.

Second, the at-will rule assumes that over time, the marketplace will regulate the parties' conduct. Conceptually, the logic behind this assumption is that an employer will not be able to continue to successfully recruit and retain talented employees if it develops a reputation for treating them poorly and discarding them willy-nilly. Presumably, the risk of working for such a company may make employees resistant about accepting employment with it. Likewise, an employee who develops a reputation for leaving an employer in the lurch may find prospective employers gun-shy about assuming the same risk. In truth, there probably is a good deal of fiction in both of these assumptions.

Third, is the assumption that both parties have the capacity to change the general rules and protect themselves from the other party's unwanted or unexpected conduct. They do this by entering into some type of agreement which particularizes many, if not all of the "whos", "whats", "whens" and "hows" of the employment relationship and the consequences that flow to each party from the termination of the relationship. For example, such an agreement may require an employer to provide advance notice before terminating an employee's employment or require specified advanced notice by the employee before the employee resigns. Or provide for severance in the event of termination by the employer without "cause".

However, and as was true with the first at-will rule above, very few employees are in a position to insist upon such a contract as a condition of accepting employment. The goal of having an agreement is sound, but the practical realities may control. Query whether you are better off without the job that you want than you are by accepting the position without the protection of an agreement? Taking the job – with full knowledge of the risks attendant in doing so without an agreement – may still be the better option. Particularly in a buyer's market where finding a job is not all that easy.

Accordingly, the employment of most employees is governed by the employment at-will rule. Unless you fall into one of the exceptions to the at-will rule discussed below, you probably are "naked", without legal rights and are employed at-will.

9.2. *Exceptions To The At-Will Rule*

As with many things in the law, the general employment at-will rule is not absolute. There are exceptions to the general at-will rule that are largely created or governed by the state law where your employment was located. For our purposes, there are three general categories of exceptions to the at-will rule on which you and your attorney should focus:

- Exceptions that are created by agreement between you and your employer.

- Statutorily created exceptions by state legislatures or the U.S. Congress.

- Exceptions created by federal and/or state courts when deciding cases before them. These types of exceptions are the rarest because courts generally are very reluctant to create rights – that is generally viewed as the province of legislatures. As the saying goes, "Courts enforce the law – they don't make them".

9.3. Why Do I Need To Think About This?

The purpose of evaluating your legal position is to determine whether your relationship with your employer places your situation within one of these exceptions to the at-will general rule – you are looking to determine whether you have any *JUICE*. If some exception applies to your situation, that probably means that there is some type of legal claim that is relevant to the termination of your employment – maybe providing you with some *JUICE*.

On the other hand, if you are unable to fit the factual circumstances surrounding your employment and separation under one of the exceptions, your status will remain "at-will". If that is the case, you are probably without legal rights arising out of the separation itself leaving you with low, or no *JUICE*!

That is why it is so important to arm yourself with a solid understanding of whether you have any legal rights. It is the basic predicate for formulating your personal business plan. Indeed, for purposes of strategic planning, it is as important for you to know that you have no rights at all as it is for you to be armed with chapter and verse of the potential array of legal wrongs that may have been committed by your employer.

If your attorney determines that you may have specific legal rights, the next step in the analysis is to try to value each of those legal rights. Ultimately, the success or failure of any business negotiation – and a negotiation involving the terms of your separation is no exception – often rises or falls on your employer's perception of the strength of the position that you bring to the bargaining table (*i.e.* how your employer evaluates its/your legal position and consequent financial and other exposure) – your *JUICE*.

10.

Deals & Agreements

The first category of exception to the employment at-will rule is the "deal" or "agreement". This exception is based upon facts that establish that you and your employer have agreed (expressly or, perhaps impliedly) to act in some manner that is inconsistent with the general at-will rule. That means that there is a legal basis to claim that you and your employer have agreed, in some respect, to limit or modify your employer's right to act on a whim, without notice and without compensation. Here, you are able to articulate something that your employer said, wrote or did that you can point to as the basis for your assertion that your employer could not do what it did (fire you) – when it did it – how it did it – or for the reasons it did it. Such agreements and deals can take many forms.

Employees constantly are amazed that they can be unceremoniously "dumped" – for no reason; without any notice; with no warning; without any severance; not without even a handshake on the way out. But if you are an at-will employee, that is all you have a legal right to expect. Accordingly, and as the saying goes: forewarned is forearmed. Next time you enter into an employment relationship, decide how much protection, and how high a comfort level you want against being "dumped" once again. Of course, the real issue is not necessarily what you want, but whether your prospective employer will agree to provide you with such protection.

Thus, in order to have a viable legal claim which falls within the "deal/agreement" exception to the at-will rule, you will have to identify and prove the particulars of a specific promise that was made to you by your employer which has been broken and caused you to suffer some demonstrable economic loss.

10.1. The Written, Fixed Term Agreement

The clearest, and generally most easily provable example of an "agreement" or "deal" which falls within this exception is the written, fixed term contract. That's because there is a paper trail that reflects the relevant terms of the "deal". In addition to the final version, there also may be relevant correspondence, electronic communications and earlier drafts of the final agreement which provide clarity to the terms. The formality of the document (*i.e.* formal agreement with "Whereas" clauses; a letter; a handwritten, informal memorandum; a "term sheet") is less important than what the document says and the clarity with which it says it.

The written fixed term contract usually provides that your employment will commence on a specified date (or event) and continue to a later, also specified date or event (*i.e.* until a change in control).

Examples:

"Your employment will commence on January 1st and continue through December 31st."

or

> "Your employment will commence upon your satisfactory completion of the Company's standard pre-hire tests and will continue until the closing of any transaction in which a majority of the issued and outstanding common stock of the Company is purchased under circumstances more fully described below . . . ."

or

> "Your employment will commence on January 1st and continue as long as your performance is satisfactory."

The underlying predicate of the at-will rule is that your employer had no obligation to make a promise to you of continued employment through the specified date or event. You employer was free to hire you and retain the unfettered right to fire you at any time. However, if your employer entered into an agreement with you which limited its rights, the law generally will enforce that promise – assuming that a court can identify the controlling date or contingency from the agreement. Difficulties often arise where the triggering contingency is tied to the occurrence of a specific event, as contrasted with a specific date, because of a dispute as to whether the specified event has occurred (*i.e.* "your employment will continue as long as the company is 'profitable'").

Since the fixed term agreement is a creation of negotiations between the parties and purports to evidence their intentions, the parties also can agree to circumscribe or limit required performance. This is accomplished by inserting other, agreed upon events or termination rights in the agreement that give either party the right to terminate the agreement early and prior to the specified end date of the agreement. These types of provisions do not eliminate or void the agreement – they simply more narrowly define the deal. Once again, however, the devil is in the details. Is the contingency subjective or objective?

Examples:

A written, fixed term employment contract specifies a start date of January 1st and an end date of December 31st. The agreement may also provide for termination before December 31st under any of the following circumstances:

- ▶ In the event of your death

- ▶ In the event of your disability (which is a term which may/should be defined in the agreement along with various qualifications accompanying the definition)

- ▶ "Cause" – which also may/should be defined in the agreement

- Upon specified advance notice without cause: *i.e.* "upon 60 days written notice by Company to employee" (and vice versa)

- Failure to achieve specified goals or benchmarks

- Change in control (subject to definition)

- Pursuant to the terms of a retirement plan

- Failure to give timely notice of exercise of option for renewal of agreement for an additional specified term

The above are only some of the more common examples of an employer's reservation of rights. In fact, lawyers possess a limitless ability to draft creative contract provisions that are intended to protect a company's (its client's) interests. Of course, both parties have to agree to such provisions when the contract is negotiated but the employer generally has the stronger hand in such negotiations.

Note that it is possible that the "term" of employment (*e.g.* 12, 24, 36 . . . months) may be extended by operation of law depending upon the law of the state that governs the agreement. You should explore with your attorney whether your continued employment following the end of the initial term under the employment agreement creates a legally recognized extension of the agreement for some additional period even in the absence of a new agreement between you and your employer (*i.e.* if you have a 1 year contract and continue working after the end of the first year, does the law provide that the contract has automatically been renewed for an additional 1 year).

A word of caution. The existence of a document or writing may only be the starting point. Even careful lawyers may not anticipate all contingencies when drafting the agreement and it may be silent as to the only contingency which now matters. Moreover, even the slightest ambiguity in contract language can make the most austere lawyer giddy. One need only refer to the thousands of volumes of law books containing tens of thousands of reported court decisions involving disputes over the meaning of contract language to appreciate that reality.

One final word. You are undoubtedly familiar with the saying that "an agreement is not worth the paper that it's written on". That's somewhat hyperbolic, but there is some truth to that because contracts and agreements are not what lawyers call "self-enforcing". That is a fancy way of saying that it may not matter how clear your rights are under a contract. No matter how inviolate, irrevocable and absolute those rights may be, neither you, nor your attorney, can force your employer to live up to the deal it made with you. Only a court of law has that power.

As a result, you are necessarily relying, in large measure, upon the good faith of your employer which, given your current situation, may not be all that comforting. Even the best of intentions when the agreement was originally signed do not necessarily hedge against the fact that times change; expectations change; conditions change; and the relevant players change. Your "rights" may not change, but your employer's willingness to deliver on those rights may. Or it may simply have a different institutional understanding of the terms of the agreement.

10.2. Verbal Deals And Agreements

The written, fixed term contract represents only one end of the continuum along which a "deal" or "agreement" may exist. Verbal promises, assurances, representations or guarantees lie at the other end of the "deal" spectrum:

Examples:

- ▶ "You are guaranteed employment for at least one year".

- ▶ "You will have a job as long as the product line stays above the following sales level . . . ."

- ▶ "You will have a job as long as the company stays independent".

- ▶ "You will have a home with this company as long as I am in charge".

Such verbal "deals" and "agreements" can be as fully enforceable as the written, fixed term deal. Proving who said what, to whom, and when is an entirely different matter. But, subject to adequate proof of the terms of the deal, the law may well enforce verbal promises made by your employer to you during the pre-employment phase of the hiring process or even such promises made to you after you started work and during the life of your employment relationship.

As noted, enforceability of verbal agreements likely will depend upon your ability to prove the particulars. Indeed, it is often difficult to distinguish between an employer's positive – and even glowing – "spin", hopeful anticipation, forecast, prediction, aspiration, and expectation, and the point at which the line is crossed into enforceable promise. Your lawyer should be able to assist in identifying where that line is drawn under the circumstances of your situation.

Example 1:

- "You will have a job with this company as long as I am in charge".

vs.

- "I hope you will have a home with this company as long as I am in charge".

The first is a reasonably clear commitment: you "will" have a job. Note however, that while it may not matter, there may be some ambiguity as to what it means to be "in charge" and what the "job" will be. Here, there is no firm end date of the "term" of the agreement; rather the term is defined by the occurrence of an event: the promise of a job ends when the promising person is no longer "in charge". Contrast that with the second statement which is just an expression of "hope" – no promise.

Example 2:

> ▶ "Congratulations. I am offering you the position of Head of the Widget Division starting January 1st. You will hold that position for at least 1 year.

> ▶ "Congratulations. I am offering you a senior position with the Company. My current plan is to create a Widget Division starting January 1st and make you the Head.

The first is a clear promise: the position is defined along with the start date and minimum period that you will hold the position. The second, however, has no term (start **and** end date) nor does it identify the "senior position" at which your employment is supposed to commence. Most important, the second contains no promise that you will ever be made Head of the Widget Division – there is no existing Widget Division and no promise to create one within any specified period of time (or ever). Moreover, the statement is even ambiguous as to whether you have been promised to be made Head if such a Division is created (*i.e.* does the "current plan" apply to creating the Division, to make you Head, or both?).

• • •

Proof of the details of a verbal agreement often present complex legal and factual considerations. For example, there often is a dispute about whether a particular conversation ever took place, or who said what to whom. Even where everyone agrees that a conversation took place, the participants may have different recollections about what was said. Recollections may blur over time, even assuming good faith on both sides of the dispute. Things get only more complicated when participants in such conversations are long gone by the time the issue becomes ripe. Obtaining cooperation from such persons may be difficult.

Moreover, the difficulty in proving the terms of a verbal agreement is a separate issue from whether the verbal agreement will be enforced by a court. Enforcement does not necessarily follow even where you are able to definitively prove the terms of the verbal agreement. One limiting factor is a legal rule intended to limit the potential for fraud – a false claim about the existence and/or terms of a purported oral agreement. In the context of employment agreements, most states have rules requiring that some such agreements must be in writing in order to be enforceable. This rule commonly is referred to as the *Statute of Frauds*. Your attorney should be able to advise you whether any verbal promises that were made to you can survive a challenge under this rule.

While the *Statute of Frauds* is a commonly recognized limitation on the enforceability of verbal contracts, the applicable legal standard may vary from state-to-state. As a general rule, however, the law of most jurisdictions limits enforceability to verbal agreements which, by their terms, are capable of being performed within one year of the making of the agreement. Thus, most states will not enforce a purported unconditional verbal agreement to employ you for a fixed term of 36 months – it cannot be performed within 1 year. Contrast that example with the one above: "You will have a job with this company as long as I am in charge". That could be 1 month, 3 months, 5 years etc. and therefore potentially enforceable. The key is that it is capable of being performed within 1 year even if it does not turn out that way. These are complex legal issues with lots of nuances that have generated legions of court cases that address these issues.

10.3. Employer Promulgated Rules

Between the two ends of the "deal" continuum (the written contract and the verbal deal), you may find that employee handbooks, personnel manuals, corporate rules, regulations and guidelines sometimes are a rich source of rights that have been unilaterally bestowed upon you by your employer. Some such documents may contain explicit limitations on the employer's exercise of its "at-will" right to terminate your employment:

Example:

> "In the event your performance is deemed to be deficient, you will be given specific standards you are required to meet and will be given at least 90 days in which to do so. At the end of that 90 day period, the Company will re-evaluate your performance...."

Depending upon the governing state law, the foregoing limitation may create a window of 90 days of promised continued employment and an enforceable limitation on the employer's right to terminate your employment prior to expiration of the 90 day remediation period.

Just as frequently, however, the same manuals and rules contain waivers and disclaimers that explicitly state that the manual or handbook creates no contractual or enforceable rights. These disclaimers generally reiterate that your employment is at-will and, despite all of the flowery provisions in the employee manual that may give the appearance of rights, the manual explicitly says – somewhere, or in multiple places – that there are no enforceable "deals" or "agreements". In other words, employers often promulgate employee manuals that contain a host of rules and regulations that it expects employees to follow while, at the same time, clearly providing that the company does not intend to be bound by any of its own rules.

The at-will rule also has applicability to compensation and benefits. As an at-will employee, the law generally only requires that you be paid the statutory minimum wage and (if you are not an exempt employee) overtime pay. Thus, benefits such as sick leave, personal leave, vacation, holiday pay and severance (to name only a few) are generally deemed to be gratuities provided by the employer on a voluntary basis. If your employer does so, it is offering benefits in excess of what the law minimally requires.

Except for certain benefits such as pensions which are governed by federal law, most of the rules that apply to these other benefits are governed by state law and each state has its own rules. By definition, if a benefit offered to you by your employer is deemed to be a gratuity in the eyes of the law, you have no enforceable legal right to the benefit as a "deal" or "agreement" exception to the "at-will" rule. As a consequence, and as was true concerning an employer's reservation of rights to terminate a fixed term employment agreement, your employer also is free to unilaterally establish whatever eligibility conditions and requirements it likes as a condition of providing the benefit and can generally cancel the benefit whenever it wants.

However, while an employer may not be obligated to provide these benefits to begin with, if the employer makes a promise to do so, the law will enforce that promise. By way of example, it is not uncommon for a sick leave policy to require medical documentation for absences of a specified duration due to illness. Unless sick leave is required by law, the employer can condition the granting of such leave upon this kind of documentation.

Likewise with respect to an employer's requirement that a separating employee sign a general release (discussed below) in exchange for severance or other separation benefits. Unless the employer is obligated by law to provide severance (or other benefit), it can set whatever non-discriminatory eligibility standards it wants.

One of the more interesting and complex legal issues arise when an employer tries to change the rules after you have continued your employment in reliance upon the old rules. Suppose your employer had a longstanding severance policy that provided for 2 weeks of severance pay for each year of service plus employer paid health insurance until you find a new job. The severance policy is limited to employees who are terminated without cause.

After working for the company for 15 years, your employer changed the policy to provide for only 1 week of severance per year of service and no post-termination health insurance. It may even have done so in anticipation of an impending downsizing in workforce. This change in policy raises legal issues which should be investigated by counsel familiar with the laws of the state in which you work. Are you entitled to benefits calculated under the old rule? Or under the new rule only? Or under the old rule until it changed and then the less generous benefits after the new rule was implemented?

Your ability to assemble a comprehensive set of employment documents as well as a detailed chronology of events will better enable a lawyer to determine whether an enforceable "agreement" or "deal" can be identified. If so, your *JUICE* will likely increase. If not, all is not lost – onto the next exception to the at-will rule.

11.

Statutorily Created Rights

The second class of exception to the at-will rule can be found in various federal, state and local laws. Employment related laws have become quite broad touching upon such areas (by way of example) as wages, health, safety, pension/retirement, insurance, and discrimination. Many of these laws also protect employees from retaliation because the employee makes a complaint involving a substantive legal right or asserting that the employee's legal rights may have been violated.

While the "agreement" or "deal" exception discussed above looks principally to the "when" of what happened (the timing of the termination in a fixed term contract) or the "what" of what happened (had the defined contingency or event taken place; did the conduct at issue justify termination), this second class of exception looks principally at the "why" of what happened – the motivation behind the conduct as contrasted with the fact of the conduct itself. By and large, statutory provisions relevant to the employment relationship address terminations and other job related actions that cross the line not solely because the event took place, but because the reason or motivation behind the employer's action is proscribed by law.

Legislative bodies that enact employment legislation may exist at 3 or more levels, depending upon where you reside and/or your place of employment. On the federal level, Congress tends to pass legislation intended to be more "macro" in nature, leaving the smaller, more individualized issues for administrative rule making or for the states and localities. It is not unusual to find that a state or locality has enacted legislation that is similar to federal law that addresses the same issue, only with broader coverage or more expansive remedies. Unless the federal law has precluded the states from enacting legislation on the same subject matter, employees generally are entitled to the benefits of the federal, state or local law that accords the employee the greatest rights.

However, legislation – whether federal, state or local – is only the starting point for employment law rights. Significant legislation often delegates rule-making authority to various executive branch agencies charged with enforcement of these laws. By way of example, these might include the federal Department of Labor, Equal Employment Opportunities Commission and state and local government agencies or departments that are responsible for dealing with these issues.

Thus, it is not unusual for a fairly short piece of federal legislation to be followed by pages upon pages of federal regulations interpreting the new legislation. These administrative rules go through a process of promulgation, public input, revision and ultimately final form, all of which sometimes can take years. The same is true on the state and local level, although the form and process tends to be less protracted.

And then, of course, the judiciary has the final (or maybe only the penultimate) say as to exactly what each law and regulation says and means. "Final" – if everyone is satisfied with the court's ruling. "Penultimate" – because the legislature can always change the law if it is not happy with the court's decision.

In addition to providing legal guidance as to what a law means, courts may also decide whether the law is constitutional. And, where the issue involves regulations promulgated by an administrative agency, a court may have to decide whether the agency had the right and authority to issue the regulations (*i.e.* whether the agency exceeded the mandate and scope of the law under which the rules were issued).

Sometimes, years later, parts or even the entire law and/or regulations at issue are declared unconstitutional or otherwise defective and thrown out by a court. That may start the process over, only this time – since it may be years later – the composition of the legislature and executive branch may have changed. That may result in significant differences in new, replacement legislation and regulations – which may start the process of judicial review all over again. And perhaps with different judges deciding the issue this time.

There are many different governmental agencies that perform quasi-judicial functions and have jurisdiction to hear cases arising under some of these laws. Various levels of state and federal courts may have jurisdiction along with various governmental administrative agencies charged with investigating violations of the law and taking enforcement action to remedy violations.

And then it gets more complicated: federal and state courts operate within their own defined judicial district. Lower state and federal courts are all free to ignore the wisdom of their sister courts in other judicial districts or states and issue their own legal pronouncements until the issue has been heard by a higher court in that jurisdiction. Sometimes the highest court in several judicial districts don't agree with each other. Then it is possible that there will be no clear answer until the matter is resolved by the state's highest court or even by the United States Supreme Court years and years later.

After all is said and done, the lower courts then have to try to figure out what the Supreme Court said and meant. One would hope that there would be some consistency to these interpretations. But even here, history suggests that such a "hope" is often unsatisfied.

11.1. *A Word About The Discrimination Laws*

As noted above, the discrimination laws are only one subset of the universe of employment laws. While this Handbook is not intended to be a primer through the thicket of discrimination laws – and there are many – a few words are needed. As you can imagine, every nuance and aspect of each term and provision of each such law has been the subject of endless regulatory rule-making, litigation and judicial interpretation.

There are volumes, upon volumes, of judicial decisions interpreting such basic issues as "who is an employee"; "what is an employer"; "what is employment" and "who is covered by the law"? Beyond that, there also are countless court decisions interpreting the scope of each right under each of these laws; and more decisions yet deciding upon appropriate remedies. It is no small wonder that there are sub-specialties among the employment law bar that deal only with these narrow rights.

Claims of violation of the anti-discrimination laws are the most common statutory exceptions to the "at-will" rule. Legislation prohibiting employment discrimination exists on the federal, state and, in many jurisdictions, local levels. Each law needs to be individually analyzed to determine the scope of coverage and prohibited conduct.

For example:

- A company may have too few employees to be covered under one law, but enough to be covered under another.

- You may be an "employee" under one law but not under another.

Thus, an employee may be protected under one law, but not under another, from adverse employment action based upon age, race, religion, national origin, sex, gender, sexual preference or orientation, religion, disability, veteran status or ethnicity – to name just a few of the recognized protected statuses. That is because each legislative body decides the statuses it wants to protect. For example, a victim of sexual preference discrimination (fired because he/she is gay), may have statutory rights under the laws of the particular state and/or city in which he/she works but not under federal law.

In order to have a viable claim of discrimination under most of these laws, you generally need to satisfy four essential predicates which are presented here in shorthand.

First, you must fall within one of the classes of individuals that the law seeks to protect – you are of a certain age, sex, religion, etc. It generally is not difficult to determine whether you are a member of a protected class.

Second, you must have suffered some type of adverse employment action. There has been a lot of litigation over the issue of what type of employer conduct satisfies this requirement. Involuntary termination of employment undoubtedly does.

Third – and here's the hard part – you have to be able to prove that there is a nexus between the first and second prongs; that your protected status played a role in the adverse action. Thus, just being 65 years of age; or just being African-American; or just being gay; or just being this or that (some status protected by law) is not enough. Nor is it enough to have been summarily fired. Rather, proof that your status "played a role in"; "motivated"; "was responsible for" (to name only several of the standards applied by various courts) will be required.

The fourth element deals with damages. You should be able to establish that you have suffered some compensable injury. The law does not compensate for every conceivable loss. In time of crisis, your visceral reaction may be to assume that the degree of your suffering and loss will carry the day in prevailing upon your legal claim. Not so. Only after you have proven your protected status, and proven that you have suffered some legally recognizable wrong does the amount of your loss come into play.

This is important. The degree to which you have suffered as a result of the termination of your employment – no matter how severe – does not define whether your legal rights have been violated. Rather, you first must establish that your legal rights have been violated by your employer's actions or conduct. Only if you are able to meet that burden do you go to the next step to determine the remedies that the law affords you for the violation.

Sadly, it does not matter (at least to the blinders of justice) that you could not pay your mortgage and lost your home; or that your spouse left you; or that you were embarrassed because you could not make the minimums at the "Club" last summer. The loss does not create or define the right; instead, the loss is a measure of damages *only* if you have a right to begin with and that right has been violated.

Just a note: many terminated employees are so outraged by their employer's conduct that they want compensation for the emotional trauma or distress they have suffered. Leaving the issue of proof aside for the moment, some statutes provide for such compensation. Most do not. Moreover, the bar to establish a common law claim of "intentional infliction of emotional distress" is quite high – the standard usually involves some variation of "conduct that shocks the public conscience". You may think that the conduct was that bad, but don't be surprised if a court has a different view.

11.2. *Other Types Of Statutory Claims*

In addition to the employment discrimination laws, there also are other federal, state and local laws that impose limitations on an employer's conduct. Examples of these include whistleblower laws (adverse employment action because you have reported or have threatened to disclose wrongdoing); laws governing the use of lie detector (*i.e.* polygraph) devices in the workplace; laws regulating plant closing and large scale layoffs; family and medical leave laws; disability and workers' compensation laws. . . .

And the list goes on. Experienced counsel will be able to identify whether any of these laws accord you protection based upon your situation.

12.

Public Policy Considerations

The third, and by far narrowest exception to the employment at-will rule is judicially created and involves limited exceptions based upon "public policy". Start with the assumption that most courts are reluctant to create a right that does not already exist in statute or common law.

Generally, the courts are of the view that the legislature is the better place for creating such a "right" and, if the legislature had wanted do so it certainly knows how. As the cry against courts "making law" rather than "enforcing the law" becomes louder, you should expect even less judicial receptivity to recognizing public policy exceptions to the at-will rule.

As a result, these judicially created public policy exceptions are limited in scope to only those circumstances where the courts cannot help but intervene – and they will do so only because there is some perceived overriding public policy that a court thinks must be vindicated. As the saying goes, 'hard cases make bad law.'

As unfair and outrageous as the circumstances surrounding your situation may be, and no matter how bad the consequences may be, you are not likely to fall within an existing or newly created "public policy" exception to the at-will rule. Again, your counsel will be able to guide you in evaluating whether you have a potential "public policy" case. These potential rights generally are governed by state, rather than federal law.

13.

Constructive Termination

The literature and cases are peppered with the concept of "constructive termination". This is a category of cases which falls in the 'gray' area of literal voluntary resignation but which, in fact, is actually a case of forced resignation.

What this means is that your employer may not have spoken the magic words: "you're fired", but your employer's conduct has placed you in such an untenable position that the law recognizes that you have no choice but to resign – not an actual, but a "constructive" termination.

In other words, you walk away from a job that you would not otherwise have left had it not been for your employer's actions. Just being miserable at work is not enough. Nor is being required to work days or shifts that you hate. Or because nobody likes you. Rather, the situation created or permitted by your employer to exist needs to be so serious that there is legally recognized justification for you to decide not to continue in the job.

Constructive termination can provide you with the same level of protection and rights discussed above relating to actual termination. However, it is the event or circumstances which ended with your involuntary resignation that will determine whether you have rights that have been violated. You have no more or better rights because you are forced out; the question will be whether you have any less. Accordingly, if the facts and circumstances surrounding your separation do not give rise to a right on your part, it does not matter if you have been fired or you have quit.

Part Three

Moving From Theory To Action

Part Three addresses some of the practical considerations involved with attempting to negotiate additional compensation and benefits from your employer now that you have an understanding of how much leverage you can bring to the process.

Negotiation is an art form, not a science. It takes skill combined with technical expertise combined with temperament. And luck. Great lawyers are not necessarily great negotiators and conversely, great negotiators might be weak lawyers.

At its core, a successful negotiation requires a strategic plan. It is hard to negotiate on the fly. This Part also discusses how to integrate the information you have gathered so far into a sound negotiating strategy.

14.

Getting Ready To Negotiate

By now, you hopefully have armed yourself with a basic understanding of your legal rights and have assembled the requisite arsenal: documents, information, facts, theory and counsel if you have decided you need or want legal representation. You have measured any separation benefits that have been offered to you against a reasonable valuation of any rights you might have.

If counsel has advised you that you are an at-will employee with no cognizable legal rights, any package offered to you ultimately must be weighed against that standard; not just against what you think is "fair", "reasonable" or "equitable". "Fairness" is not a standard that the law objectively embraces, although fairness and equity may be appropriate guides through the negotiating process.

Now that you have an idea of the *JUICE* you may bring to negotiations with your former employer, the next step to a successful negotiation is an assessment of the type of negotiator you are going to be. Particularly at this stage, critical self-analysis is not easy. In fact, many people are inclined to avoid this sometimes painful introspection and deal with it another day. But this is an extremely important step. It is important because it goes to the very heart of your strategic plan – both means and end. If you cannot, or do not properly evaluate your strengths and weaknesses as a negotiator, the means become muddled and the ends therefore become more distant and possibly elusive.

14.1. Choosing Your Negotiating Posture

There are two basic paths down which you can pursue negotiations with your employer. Since negotiations typically are "off-the-record", the discussions and give-and-take generally are not usable in any litigation that may ensue if you and your employer cannot informally resolve matters.

Negotiations are about signals, signs, body language, phrasing and the like. A misreading by either party can cause the negotiations to become derailed or an outright failure. Thus, the path you elect to pursue should reflect an educated balancing of all of these considerations including a reasoned decision as to:

- ▶ the kind of negotiator you want to be;
- ▶ the kind of negotiator you are capable of being;
- ▶ the kind of negotiator your employer is likely to be; and
- ▶ the upside and downside of the means selected to achieve the target end game.

While there may not be a clear right answer or option, there may well be a wrong one. If you fail to identify avenues of potential failure before you begin, you will start the process with one hand tied behind your back. Doing so also means that you are not starting with a sound strategic plan – you have decided to "wing it" and takes things as they come. That makes it significantly more difficult to deal with these issues when they are staring you in the face and you may have far less wiggle room, perhaps because you have already backed yourself into a corner. You may also be short on time within which to make a decision.

Finally, and before you start down either the "*Aw C'mon*" or "*Stick-Em Up*" path of negotiation, you should carefully value each of the benefits that you are considering pursuing. The result may suggest the path better suited to your end game.

From your employer's perspective, there generally is a cost attributable to each benefit in negotiations. The package – or the amount that the company is prepared to spend – is not limitless. Thus, and as is discussed elsewhere, you should avoid asking for benefits that may turn out to provide you with little actual cash or benefit. You may get what you ask for at the cost of other, more important or valuable things!

For those with basic technological skills, you should be able to prepare basic spreadsheets which will reflect various valuations depending upon certain relevant variables.

For example, if the retirement plan in which you are a participant has a formularized approach to benefits and vesting (*i.e.* benefits based upon a combination of age and years of service), you should first determine whether you are at the point where you have maximized your possible benefits under the plan. If you have not, you should graph (or ask the company's human resource or pension consultants do so) a variety of "what-if" scenarios. "What-if" I had (or were credited with) "X" number of additional years of service (which would bring me to age 55/65) – by how much would my monthly retirement benefit change? "What-if" the company adopts an early retirement program (as may have been rumored) that provides for enhanced retirement benefits above what has been given to me in a separation agreement I sign?

The calculation of the various "what-ifs" may be mathematically imprecise, but close enough to allow you to determine whether the benefit is worth pursuing. To the extent that additional years of service credit and/or added years to your age only marginally affect your monthly retirement benefit under present assumptions, the cost of persuading the company to provide such "bridge" coverage may be disproportionately large to the value of the new benefit levels.

Likewise with respect to such other benefits as stock options that have yet to vest or are currently "out of the money". Negotiating accelerated vesting of unvested options or mitigating the effect of a scheduled forfeiture under an option plan may result in a 'benefit' that is not worth having – you now have the options, but they have little or no cash value because the company's stock price is so depressed and isn't likely to recover very much during the life of the option. That is particularly true with new-age companies with tenuous financials; in fact, that may be the very reason you are reading this.

For both you and your employer, the negotiating process is about tomorrow, not yesterday – your financial cushion while you look for your next position and your employer's closure of yesterday's relationship with you so that it does not have to address it again, potentially in litigation.

14.2. The "Aw C'mon" Approach

The first type of negotiating option can colloquially be referred to as the *"Aw C'mon"* approach. *"Aw C'mon"* is a low-keyed appeal to your employer's sense of fair play, equity, reasonableness and gratitude for all that you have done for the company: *"Aw C'mon"* this isn't fair; *"Aw C'mon"* I was a great employee and delivered great bottom line numbers; *"Aw C'mon"* the economy is terrible and it will take me forever to find another job; *"Aw C'mon"* I'm already up to my ears in debt . . . .

The *"Aw C'mon"* approach asks your employer to do something for you that it has no legal obligation to do (*i.e.* your lawyer has not identified any legal theory or claim arising out of the termination of your employment). *"Aw C'mon"* also asks your employer to do something which, based upon its original separation package, it has already indicated that it is not inclined to do.

In other words, you are asking your former employer to accord you a gratuity based upon the strength of your historical relationship. As a result, an *"Aw C'mon"* negotiation has a low likelihood of success.

14.3. The "Stick-Em Up" Approach

The second, alternate approach to negotiations can been inartfully described as *"Stick-Em Up"*. This is not pejorative; it is short-hand for what lawyers do best. This approach relies upon a forceful and aggressive (even if done with a smile) use of an available legal theory to raise your employer's level of consciousness and concern. The goal is to induce your employer to reach a financial agreement with you that brings closure to its relationship with you without litigation.

Virtually every terminated employee believes that the "wrongs" committed by their employer create a monster legal claim that is a "slam dunk" and worth a fortune. Notwithstanding clients' confidence, very few lawyers are ever lucky enough to see a massively valued slam dunk case anytime in their careers. Especially in the area of employment law.

If there is no available legal claim upon which to rely, you are left with being an *"Aw C'mon"* negotiator. It may not carry the same punch, but you have to live with the cards you are dealt. Even where your lawyer has identified a potential legal claim, it is not automatic that you proceed down the *"Stick-Em Up"* path. For a variety of reasons, you may decide not to involve a lawyer or are more comfortable with the softer, *"Aw C'mon"* approach. Doing so should reflect a thoughtful, knowing decision to forego *"Stick-Em Up"* in favor of *"Aw C'mon"*.

14.4. Are "Aw C'mon" And "Stick-Em Up" Inconsistent?

The decision as to which approach to use is important because the *"Aw C'mon"* and *"Stick-Em Up"* paths are fundamentally inconsistent with each other, even if not mutually exclusive as a matter of law. Thus, there is nothing in the law that limits your right to first go down the *"Aw C'mon"* path and then decide, when you reach the other end, that you are not satisfied with the results of the negotiations and then attempt to go down the *"Stick-Em Up"* path. The law is replete with instances of inconsistent or alternative argument.

With that in mind, you are likely to be tempted to attempt *"Aw C'mon"* on your own to see how far it gets you. You would not be alone in thinking it's worth doing so just to see how much more you can extract from your employer without involving – and paying – a lawyer. But this is a risky gambit. If you are not satisfied with the results of your own *"Aw C'mon"* negotiation, you likely will find that it is difficult to then engage counsel for a *"Stick-Em Up"* negotiation. Unless you have a great legal case.

But even then, there are 3 basic reasons why the dual path approach is difficult. First, by negotiating with your employer using an appeal to its sense of equity and fair play (*"Aw C'mon"*), you undoubtedly will moderate your requests for additional compensation in an attempt to avoid getting the door slammed in your face or ticking off your employer by making a demand for a lot more money. By doing so, you may have effectively transmitted your bottom line. That makes it difficult for a lawyer to then enter the picture and substantially raise the "asking" price on your behalf.

Second, once you have gone to the well on your own behalf, a lawyer may want greater compensation due to the greater risk he is undertaking in your representation (*i.e.* it is now more difficult and less likely to successfully negotiate a settlement).

And third, the person with whom you are negotiating may not be willing to go to the "well" again for your lawyer.

15.

"Aw C'mon" Negotiations

Before exploring the *"Aw C'mon"* negotiating option in greater detail, a few words about what this approach is *not*. Since *"Aw C'mon"* is an appeal to your employer's sense of fairness and equity, the threat of a lawsuit would be misplaced. Indeed, if there is a basis for the assertion of a legal claim, why aren't you pursing the *"Stick-Em Up"* path of negotiations? And, in the absence of a viable legal claim, such a threat usually is counterproductive. No matter how you couch it, a frivolous claim (which such a threat would be without any basis in law to support the claim) invites an already wary employer to change its stance from defense to offense.

Moreover, if you advance a frivolous claim, a reasonable employer and its own counsel will likely conclude that either your lawyer does not know the law; or that you are prepared to make things up (which tends to scare a company); or that you are bluffing and probably lack resolve; or that ultimately you will have the wisdom not to pursue such a claim. In any event, it is an approach that appears borne of frustration and will be easily seen as such and will likely cause you significantly more harm than any potential good.

Given the inherent nature of the *"Aw C'mon"* approach, it generally is done with a modest or soft touch. That means that there are no wild or outrageous demands. The approach is designed to enhance a severance package on the margin, not to rewrite the financial terms of separation on a wholesale basis. If the spread between what has been offered to you and your "demand" is within the range appropriate to the *"Aw C'mon"* approach, most sophisticated employers (and their counsel) will recognize that you are not likely to start litigation to try to recover the marginal amount you are seeking and thereby risk losing the offer that is already on the table.

By the time you factor in the attorneys' fees, income taxes and related risks inherent in litigation, the net spread would likely be too small to make sense to pursue in litigation or to find a lawyer willing to take your case. That's why you are using the *"Aw C'mon"* approach instead of having your lawyer threaten litigation.

Example:

> Your employer has offered you 6 months of severance. It would be imprudent to start an *"Aw C'mon"* negotiation by asking for 36 or more months, for example. If you did so, you likely would get no response at all. Instead, you ask for an additional 3, 4, 5 or even 6 months of severance in the exercise of prudence, hoping that such a modest request will move your employer. But what is the message to your employer from such a request? If you ask for an additional 6 months, your employer will reasonably conclude that you will settle for less – maybe an additional 1, 2 or 3 months. And if that is true, is also fair for your employer to assume that you are not likely to risk the 6 months already offered by starting a lawsuit to chase an additional few months of

severance which would have limited net value to you after taxes and attorneys' fees – assuming you win your case.

The very nature of the *"Aw C'mon"* approach relies upon the existence of a reservoir of good will and your employer's sense of generosity, both of which limit the upside potential of the *"Aw C'mon"* approach. It's one thing for management to explain its decision to settle a potential, legitimate (even if weak) legal claim by paying additional severance; it is quite another to explain a decision to raid the corporate coffers just because you are a nice guy.

15.1. Who Should Do The Negotiations?

As a result of the inherent limitations to the *"Aw C'mon"* approach, these negotiations generally are not appropriate for a lawyer to undertake. It is a process that is uniquely suited to the individual employee – you. Lawyers deal with legal rights and wrongs. They are trained to craft legal theories that they can package and spin to a client's best advantage. In other words, lawyers are best at leveraging a client's legal position for the client's financial benefit.

Moreover, there is real practical risk in having a lawyer approach your employer with an *"Aw C'mon"* demand for increased compensation. Imagine the following scenario:

> You consult a lawyer who advises you that he cannot identify any legal rights arising out of the termination of your employment. Nevertheless, you believe that the severance package offered

to you is woefully inadequate. Moreover, you are quite sure that if your employer gets a 'lawyer's letter' it will substantially increase the severance it is offering – either because you are a good guy; or because you were a heck of an employee; or because it does not want any adverse publicity.

Your lawyer then writes a letter to your employer's human resource professional and proposes a discussion concerning the severance package. The company's human resource professional will likely, and prudently, refer your letter to the company's attorney (either its in-house counsel or an outside law firm that represents the company in employment law matters).

After some due diligence to gather the facts, the company's lawyer calls your lawyer and asks the basis for the demand for increased severance. Since your lawyer is ethically bound not to advance a frivolous claim on your behalf, your lawyer responds by regaling all of your virtues and good work for the company.

The likely response from the company's lawyer: 'yeah, so what'? "That's why the company so handsomely paid your client during the years he worked for the company".

In sum, lawyers are not trained to do *"Aw C'mon"* – it lacks *JUICE*. Lawyers do *"Stick-Em Up"*. If the lawyer cannot articulate some basis for a legal claim, he is acting like a fish out of water. It doesn't work.

On the other hand, it is perfectly natural for you to make such an appeal on your own behalf. You may not be successful, but such an approach presents a wholly different picture to your employer than sending a lawyer in to do battle without any ammunition.

15.2. The Risk of Getting Lost In The "Group"

Don't be surprised if the lower expectations that the "*Aw C'mon*" process holds are even harder to meet when you are part of a large/larger group of employees being separated. That's because individual (or small group) terminations generally are more easily negotiated than a large or "mass" reduction in force or layoff.

The larger the number of employees who are impacted by a reduction in force being implemented by your employer, the more reluctant your employer may be to create exceptions to its severance policy or the "standard" separation package it has developed for this reduction in workforce. Exceptions may raise legal risks that the company does not want to address.

Sometimes, it simply is easier, cleaner and less risky for a company to treat all separating employees similarly. Your employer has more of a reason *not* to adjust its offer to you than it has for doing so.

15.3. Your Place In The "Food Chain"

Even if you are able to negotiate on an individual basis (*i.e.* you are not part of a group layoff), there is an inverse relationship between the wrung you occupy in the corporate hierarchy and the likelihood of a successful *"Aw C'mon"* negotiation. As you get lower in the corporate food chain, there are fewer corporate executives who have any real authority to go to bat for you. There may also be no one with a personal incentive to do so. Indeed, a superior who goes to bat for you may have to explain to his superiors why he is advocating doing something for a former employee that the company is not required to do. It should be obvious that a superior will be even less willing to do so if your termination was due to performance or something other than mere downsizing.

Conversely, the more senior you are, the more likely you are to have forged personal relationships with senior management or members of the Board of Directors that you might be able to leverage to your advantage. Your situation will more easily rise or fall on its own rather than being lumped together with many other employees.

15.4. Leveraging Your "Aw C'mon" Appeal To The "Max"

At its core, the *"Aw C'mon"* appeal needs to provide your employer with a compelling reason to change its mind and adjust your separation package. As part of your strategy to frame your appeal, you certainly should highlight all of the things that you did for your employer over the many years of blood, sweat and tears. Point to the cost savings you created; the innovations you implemented; and your corporate good citizen activities. You can express concern about the job market in a tough economic climate or the difficulty you will have in finding a new job "at your age" or at this time of year. But, even where your employer recognizes the truth of these appeals, don't be surprised if management considers yesterday's compensation, bonus, options and the like to be adequate reward to you for yesterday's services.

In sum, the *"Aw C'mon"* approach is the only viable path where you have no legal claim. But you should accept that it has a low likelihood of success because there is nothing providing a strong inducement to your employer to modify its original offer – your employer is not exposed legally and has already evidenced no inclination to do more voluntarily. In those limited instances where there is a reservoir of good will that might cause your employer to be more forthcoming, the potential rewards can best be attained through your own efforts.

Even where you have a viable legal claim, however, you may decide not to pursue the *"Stick-Em Up"* approach. But, if you still want to try to negotiate an enhanced separation package, you might try *"Aw C'mon"* plus – a combination of *"Aw C'mon"* along with the "veiled" threat of a legal claim.

You:

"I really think that the severance package you've offered is way too light. I am looking for __ additional months of severance to tide me over. I am hoping that you can do that so I don't have to get a lawyer involved."

Or

"I really think that the severance package you've offered is way too light. I am looking for __ additional months of severance to tide me over. The company has really put somebody **at my age** in a bad spot. Seems like all of the older workers are gone."

While this dual approach may be somewhat awkward, it may nevertheless be worth a try. It does not run afoul of the rule against asserting a frivolous claim but, rather, allows you to voice a concern that you have, almost as an aside.

16.

"Stick-Em Up" Negotiations

As discussed in Chapter 15, the separating employee is better suited than a lawyer to pursue an *"Aw C'mon"* negotiation. The reverse is true when it comes to the *"Stick-Em Up"* approach. Here, the lawyer is likely the better advocate for your position. The role of counsel is to develop a cogent legal theory that he spins out of a set of facts culled from a detailed debriefing with you. Webster defines "fact" as: *"a thing that has actually happened or is true."* If it were that easy, what would the lawyers do? No, as everyone understands, fact may only be true in the eyes of the beholder or when a court of law says so.

While leverage in an *"Aw C'mon"* negotiation rests upon the strength of your reservoir of good will with your employer, the leverage in a *"Stick-Em Up"* negotiation, if any, is derivative of the type of legal claim that your counsel develops and the "facts" that your lawyer can assemble in support of the legal claim. And your employer's assessment of its risk.

Don't be fooled: negotiations generally do not succeed based upon how well known your lawyer is. Lawyers develop a good reputation because of their legal acumen and their proven ability to successfully deliver on a client's goals, not as a result of a baseless threat of litigation or because a lawyer appears as a commentator on a TV or cable show.

Given a choice, most companies would prefer a non-litigated resolution of most claims. The time, cost and distraction to personnel that litigation carries can result in significant workplace disruption. At the same time, it is a mistake to assume that your employer will retreat based simply upon a threat of litigation. In fact, it would be hard to identify an employer of any significant size that has not been a defendant in employment related litigations.

Employment litigation has become so common that there are now employment practices insurance policies that provide employers with coverage for some such employment litigation and claims. Thus, while litigation is a distasteful part of doing business, it has become a part of everyday corporate life and is viewed as just another cost of doing business. Except in rare cases, you will not likely scare your employer into submission simply with the threat of a lawsuit. From its perspective – been there – done that!

16.1. *Damages: Leverage Involving A Contract Claim*

The most effective *JUICE* (the amount of leverage that you can bring to the negotiating table) comes from a lawyer's ability to articulate a legal claim that carries potential risk that your employer cannot easily quantify (*i.e.* it cannot reasonably calculate the amount of damages that might be awarded against the employer if the case went to trial and you win). As the amount of potential damages increases, the risk to the employer of litigation likewise increases.

Damages that are available for some types of claims can be readily calculated. One such type of case is a straight breach of contract case (*i.e.* a claim that some deal, arrangement or promise by your employer to you was not honored). In simplified form, damages available in a breach of contract case are valued by subtracting the value of what was actually paid or received under the contract from the value of full performance of the contract.

Contract claims generally are governed by the law of the state in which you worked unless the contract specifies that the law of a different state applies. In most states – and again, that might change depending upon what the contract itself says – the loss to you resulting for a premature termination of the contract by your employer will be reduced by amounts you earn, or could have earned if you had exercised reasonable diligence to find a new job after you were terminated. The law of some states also will reduce the amount recoverable for losses arising from a breach of contract for unemployment insurance and other benefits you receive.

Example 1:

You had a three year fixed term employment contract with a total compensation package (salary and benefits) valued at $150,000 per year ($12,500 per month). You have been fired, without cause, after 20 months. Under the purest calculation, your damages would be the value of the 16 months left under the contract – $12,500 x 16 = $200,000.

Example 2:

Same as Example 1, except that you find a job after 6 months of unemployment with a total compensation package also valued at $150,000 per year. Here, your cognizable contract damages would be the value of the 6 months that you were unemployed – $12,500 x 6 = $75,000. The law will not compensate you for the additional 10 months since you were able to eliminate any loss attributable to that period.

Example 3:

Same Example as above, except that you find a job after 6 months of unemployment with a total compensation package valued at $100,000 per year – $50,000 per year less than the value of the broken contract. Here, your cognizable contract damages would be $116,670 computed as follows: (i) the value of the 6 months that you were unemployed – $12,500 x 6 months = $75,000 plus (ii) the loss you will have for the 10 months thereafter (the difference between the value of a month's compensation under the contract ($12,500) and the compensation for your new job ($8,333): $4,167 x 10 months = $41,670.

However, note that even calculations in contract cases can get complicated. By way of example, issues may arise as to whether the termination was, in fact, a breach of the contract; whether you actively pursued a new position as required to mitigate your damages; why you took a new position that paid less than another position that was also available; whether benefits that you enjoyed while employed were lawfully eliminated by the company during the period remaining on your contract reducing the amount of your actual loss; whether the company went out of business or filed for protection under the bankruptcy laws; or the valuation of various benefits that you enjoyed while employed but which lapsed, were forfeited or terminated when your employment ended.

16.2. Damages: Leverage Involving A Discrimination Or Tort Claim

Where an employer can reasonably calculate its potential liability (with or without insurance) if it loses a case you bring in litigation, it can better evaluate how much is at risk and how much of that risk the company is willing to assume. As discussed above, the outside limits of liability in a contract case can be reasonably calculated. The employer can calculate its worst case scenario if it is required to pay you 100% of the value of the contract for the entire period from date of termination to the last day of the contract. That may limit the amount of *JUICE* you have.

Conversely, where the employer's potential liability is subject to an imprecise guesstimate – at best – an employer may be more resistant to assuming the risk of a worst case scenario you may have more *JUICE*. Add to that equation the reality that lawyers sometimes lose cases that they were confident they should win, and win cases that they should have lost. Uncertainty on both sides is a strong driver in the leverage contest.

While the outside period of liability can be identified in a contract period, the amount of time that a terminated employee with a discrimination, or other statutory or tort claim will be out of work may not be known. That means that an employer's potential liability can run for a long time. Maybe you will find a new job in a month; or maybe not for 3 months; or maybe it will take 1, 2, 3 years or longer. Your age, skills and the economy may be relevant, although not easily quantifiable variables.

In addition, you might be awarded damages for emotional distress, punitive damages and your attorneys' fees. An employer's inability to accurately quantify the potential financial downside of losing a lawsuit brought by you (even if insurance may cover some of the loss) makes it difficult for the employer to make a cost/benefit analysis. Your *Juice* is greater.

16.3. "Juice" May Be Illusory

Not every claim – even those that are well grounded in law – can be negotiated to settlement. Even if by every rational consideration your employer should be unwilling to litigate with you. By all accounts, you should have serious *Juice*.

Maybe: but for some companies, refusing to settle is a matter of principle and corporate culture: they want to be sure that all employees understand that there is no free ride. In order to make sure that the message is not lost by its workforce, this class of company meets virtually every claim with an aggressive and lengthy defense. It forces the litigating employee to fight for every inch. The intended message is clear: "Mess with the company and we will make your life miserable."

As a corollary, you may find it difficult to find a lawyer willing to take your case unless you have a strong legal claim with significant damages or you will be entitled to be compensated for your legal fees if you win after doing battle with a company with such a reputation. No lawyer wants to "win the battle but lose the war" by spending a disproportionately high amount of time litigating a case on your behalf that fails to adequately compensate the lawyer for the time he has invested in your case.

There are also cases where the employer has a fundamentally different view of the facts and/or law from the positions your lawyer is advocating and believes it cannot justify settling such a claim. Still other employers may have an institutional reason for resisting your settlement overtures including the need to stand behind management decision making. And sometimes, your demands are simply too high.

Thus, even if you think that you have lots of *JUICE;* and even if an objective evaluation of your case suggests that you do have lots of *JUICE,* you still do not control the entire process. Notwithstanding all of your *JUICE,* your former employer won't settle. You cannot force your employer to negotiate; and you cannot force your employer to settle – the best you can do under such circumstances is to take the original offer or sue.

16.4. Talk Is Cheap: An Employer May Do It For Strategic Reasons

Even an employer that is resistant to making settlements with employees as a matter of principle or corporate policy, may be receptive to an off-the-record discussion with your attorney. The employer may do so to find out what your attorney thinks he sees, the facts that he is relying upon and the legal theory(s) that he thinks are applicable to your claims. The employer may even engage in a preliminary discussion as to the amount of damages that your lawyer thinks you can achieve in litigation. Talk is cheap and your employer may be hoping to get information that may be useful later in litigation. It also is possible that your employer may learn something it did not know and change its position – unlikely, but possible.

Given the opening, your lawyer has an opportunity to lay out your position. Employers don't live in a cocoon; serious businesses have personnel consultants, human resource professionals and employment lawyers with whom they regularly consult. Most businesses try to operate within the rules. Businesses also recognize that things occasionally fall through the cracks and that sometimes an employment action should not have been taken or may even have been taken for potentially actionable reasons.

If your lawyer has an opportunity to present your claims to your employer, your employer then will have several options. Your employer can simply not respond any further – sooner or later, you will get the message. Or, once having heard your version of what happened and why your lawyer thinks it raises a legal claim, your employer can reject your claims and show your lawyer the door. Or it can investigate your claims, and then deny any wrongdoing and show your lawyer the door. Or it can investigate your claims, deny any wrongdoing, but invite your lawyer to make a "reasonable" settlement proposal just to "avoid the cost of litigation". The least likely outcome is that your employer will acknowledge wrongdoing, beg for forgiveness and offer generous compensation.

In sum, there is a direct relationship between the risk and reward of these two varied approaches to negotiations:

"Aw C'mon":	**Risk:**	Low
	Potential Reward:	Low
"Stick-Em Up":	**Risk:**	High
	Potential Reward:	Higher than "Aw C'mon"

Negotiations are not a risk free, zero-sum process. While you can try to manage and minimize the risk, you probably cannot eliminate it entirely.

17.

Getting In The Front Door or "Can We Talk . . ."

17.1. The "Do It Yourself" Negotiator

If you have decided to be your own negotiator (proceeding with discussions with your employer without a lawyer), you need to decide with whom to communicate about the terms of your separation package. This assumes that you have a choice. Sometimes, you are given a separation agreement that details the terms of the package along with a cover letter that directs you to contact a specified person with any questions, comments, etc. Of course, you are not bound by those instructions – especially as an ex-employee – but that designation may carry a message that you should carefully evaluate. As a practical matter, no one else at the company may agree or even be permitted to talk with you.

The possibilities for your initial point of contact include the human resource professional responsible for your position; your immediate boss; a more senior member of management; or a member of the Board of Directors. You will have fewer options for initial contact the more senior you are.

As a general proposition, you should try to communicate with someone with whom you have a relationship; preferably a corporate "rabbi" if you have one. If you are proceeding without counsel, you have elected the *"Aw C'mon"* approach which has, at its core, an appeal to the company's sense of fair play. As a result, it helps to negotiate with someone who you anticipate will be sympathetic.

Where you have a choice of contacts, there are strong reasons for not going directly to the most senior person available. One reason is that there is no place left for you to go once you have exhausted the good offices of that senior executive. If your "rabbi" refuses to meet with you; or shoots down any proposals you advance; or refers you to someone less senior, you may have no further avenue of appeal if you are unsatisfied with the outcome of your efforts.

Conversely, you do not want to start so low on the corporate ladder that you are negotiating with someone with no authority to make decisions or cut a deal. Start high enough that you get a fair hearing from someone with "*JUICE*", but, if possible, keep one last bite in reserve in the event you need it.

The main difference is that by going "up stream", you may preserve the opportunity to appeal to a higher authority. Going "down stream", however, effectively eliminates this possibility. Once the CEO has divested himself of this issue, you should not expect that you can call upon him again and get a second hearing. The exception of course, applies if you are so senior that there is only a President, Chief Executive Office or Board member who is more senior than you.

17.2. *Using A Lawyer To Be Your Negotiator*

Assuming that the claim preliminarily identified by your lawyer is not frivolous, and the lawyer is going to be your negotiator, you and counsel must establish a preliminary strategy.

First, you need to decide the best way to contact your employer. That's because the person initially contacted by your lawyer may be different than the person you would contact if you are going to try to negotiate yourself.

Next, you also need to identify those claims that will be advanced on your behalf; how much information will be disclosed to your employer; and what your demand (or "proposal") for settlement will be.

While the person who will be the initial point of contact is one of the most important decisions that you may make if you are handling the negotiations yourself, the decision is less important if a lawyer will be contacting your employer on your behalf. In that case, it is likely that your lawyer will be referred to, or contacted directly by the company's own counsel regardless of whom your lawyer initially attempts to contact at the company (*e.g.* your boss, or the company's human resource professional).

An exception may involve a small business that does not have an in-house counsel or an outside lawyer that the company looks to for advice and representation for employment law matters. In that case, the company may handle things differently and negotiations may take place directly with a personnel manager, human resource profession, senior company executive or business owner.

However, in the larger business setting, the increased likelihood that the employer will refer your lawyer to the company's own lawyer is not necessarily bad. Indeed, the fact that your employer will likely do so may drive the strategic plan to have your counsel initiate contact. Sometimes it is easier to resolve employment disputes between lawyers than it is between individuals who may have a direct, personal stake in the matter. Note however, that once a lawyer enters the picture for your employer, your lawyer may then be ethically constrained to talk only to the company's lawyer. That consideration should be part of the strategy mix when deciding whether you or your attorney should make the initial contact with your employer.

17.3. Selecting The Initial Contact

Presumably, your lawyer will conduct considerable due diligence involving fact development and appropriate legal research in preparation for contacting your employer. During that process, your lawyer may be able to determine the name of the company's chief in-house lawyer and the names of various outside law firms that have represented the company in its various legal matters.

Newspaper, legal research databases and internet searches may provide even more detailed information as to law firms which the company uses in various cities for specific areas of law (*i.e.* the company's employment/labor lawyers in Chicago, Los Angeles, New York, etc.). It may also disclose the type and number of reported employment lawsuits in which your employer has been involved.

If your lawyer's research discloses the name of a lawyer who has represented the company with whom he is familiar, consideration should be given to having your counsel directly contact that lawyer and by-pass all of the company's executives and human resource professionals. This approach has the advantage of potentially allowing you to pick your adversary "point-person" and someone with whom your lawyer can talk "turkey". The initial conversation might go something like this:

Your Counsel:

Hello Sue. It's Bob Barrister. How's the law been treating you. I've been following your career and I am impressed.

Company's Counsel:

Hi Bob. Nice to hear from you; keeping busy, I presume.

Your Counsel:

Absolutely. In fact, that's one of the reasons I called. I have a vague recollection that you represented XYZ Company some time ago in connection with some employment law matter.

Company's Counsel:

Good memory Bob. I received some good press from my work in that case. And, yes, I still do work for XYZ. Why do you ask?

Your Counsel:

I've been retained by an employee who is being separated from XYZ and I am really troubled by some of the circumstances. Before all hell breaks loose, I thought I might reach out to someone to see if we can find some common ground. Then, I remembered that you represented XYZ so I took a chance and called.

Company's Counsel:

Well, I am very flattered, but I haven't been contacted by XYZ concerning your client.

Your Counsel:

If you think it appropriate, perhaps you could contact your people at XYZ, let them know that I've called and see if XYZ would like you to get involved. It would be fun working on this matter together.

Company's Counsel:

Let me make some phone calls and I'll call you back.

Your Counsel:

Great. Why I don't put a tickler in my calendar to call you next week if I haven't heard from you by then so that I don't feel ignored. Bye.

Flattery does not always work, but "feeding" a potential piece of business to a lawyer usually gets their attention. It also is useful to have someone with whom you can have a candid, and less formal discussion. If it works out, so much the better; if not, you probably have not lost any ground.

17.4. Deciding Upon The Method Of Initial Contact & The "Demand Letter"

Once you have decided whether you or your attorney will initiate contact and have identified the individual who will be the initial point of contact, the next decision is the method of communication. Depending upon the circumstances and the reaction you are trying to evoke, there are real differences between making contact by way of a letter, e-mail or telephone call.

If you have elected to proceed on your own, a telephone call to your contact person is the most logical method of communication. It has the benefit of informality and, if possible, you can have a collegial, non-confrontational discussion. You also will be less concerned that you may put something in writing that you later regret or causes you a problem.

If contact is to be initiated by your attorney, the choice is less clear unless the informal lawyer-to-lawyer approach discussed above makes sense. A telephone call by your lawyer probably should be avoided unless there is a personal connection between your attorney and the company official who will be contacted. Instead, a brief letter will allow the recipient to decide whether to handle the matter personally or forward it to the company's counsel, human resources or someone else.

Inasmuch as an immediate, and irresistibly generous offer of settlement by your employer is an unlikely outcome of an initial telephone call, a letter should avoid the risk that the recipient is caught off guard and says or does something that may make that person more defensive as the process evolves. There is little value in the sneak attack approach to negotiations; sooner or later it is likely to backfire and leave you no better (and perhaps worse) than you were to begin with. Since the negotiating process is designed to induce your employer to do something it was not otherwise inclined to do, it ill-behooves you to start the process by being unduly provocative.

Thus, a letter or e-mail is most often the safest initial approach. But even sending a letter presents options. There are two schools of thought concerning the structure of the initial letter.

The first advocates for transmittal of a detailed letter. This type of letter is the classic "lawyer's letter" – it lays out the facts and circumstances giving rise to counsel's communication and outlines the various legal positions and theories that your lawyer claims creates legal liability for the employer. This letter will also generally contain a threat of litigation. It may also contain a description of the injuries and damages you have (and will) suffered along with an outline the parameters of a non-litigated settlement. Clients like the perceived power of this type of "in your face" letter. It makes clients feel as though they have someone who is aggressively advocating on their behalf.

The second type of letter is anathema to lawyers who, as a class, are overly confident in their ability to carry the day with written word. This genre is a short letter that advises your employer of your attorney's status as your representative and contains a reference to unspecified claims and issues for which counsel has been engaged. The letter then concludes with an invitation to your employer to contact your lawyer to discuss matters. Some clients are really put off by this perceived 'milk-toast' approach because they think the lawyer is not being aggressive enough and will appear weak.

That's possible, but there are several concerns raised by the first approach. First, any such detailed letter by your attorney may become a discoverable document in the context of other (or not yet existent litigation). In order to mitigate against the impact such a letter might have, the company may harden its position so that it can "explain", in a written reply, why your lawyer doesn't know what he's talking about.

Second, and equally important, is that the underlying purpose of the letter is to evoke a response and open a channel of communication and dialogue. By reciting chapter and verse of the facts and law which your lawyer asserts is applicable to your case, such a detailed letter invites – almost requires – your employer to respond with a detailed rebuttal or simple outright denial. Now what does your lawyer do? Send another letter?

In contrast, the second type of letter provides such sparse information that it hopefully appeals to the recipient's curiosity and evokes a telephone call or letter to your lawyer for more information. If that happens, the door has been opened and your skilled counsel can walk through and invite himself to an "off-the-record" meeting or telephone call to discuss your case. Sometimes, an employer responds to the shortened initial letter with a response asking for details and particulars. If so, your lawyer can decide whether to call the writer or provide the requested written response.

Despite a well-conceived strategic plan, remember that you and your lawyer do not control the entire process. If your employer does not want to talk, or insists upon a detailed written specification of claims, you will either play by your employer's rules or be left with few palatable alternatives.

You should not get anxious if the letter from your lawyer does not receive an immediate response. While it is not unheard of to receive a response to a lawyer's letter very quickly, you should assume that a minimum of two weeks (10 business days) will elapse before a response to a letter is received. Here's why: once the letter leaves your lawyer's office it has to be received by the person to whom it is directed; that person has to be in his office and not away for personal or business reasons. The recipient may need to do some homework and investigate. That takes some time. If the recipient decides to forward the letter to someone else, that likewise will take time. After forwarding, the next recipient also may not be in the office; and that person will probably want to conduct some type of informal investigation and then decide whether to pass it on to someone else like the company's counsel.

If so, there may be yet another time lapse before a response is directed to your lawyer. If all of that happens within 10 business days, things are moving along just fine. If no response is forthcoming by the end of the third week (15 business days), most lawyers will write again or contact the company in another manner. While you should always feel free to contact your lawyer to check on the status of your matter, you should not feel ignored if 2-3 weeks pass without any word.

As noted above, it is not customary to get an immediate response, but sometimes it happens. Accordingly, your lawyer should have completed his fact development and due diligence before he sends his letter to the company.

The strategic plan should be in place. The lawyer should know the facts that he is going to present and be fully fluent in the legal theories and claims he will assert. The safe approach is to assume that negotiations will begin the day after the letter leaves your lawyer's office. That way, neither you nor your lawyer will get caught unprepared.

Since leverage is the name of the game which, in some measure, is a function of perception, your lawyer should avoid being in the position of responding to a telephone call from the company (or its counsel) by saying he's not yet finished his fact development and will get back to the caller in several days. Wham! Bad message. Unless the statute of limitations is approaching, take the time to be sure that you and your lawyer are ready to proceed before your lawyer's letter leaves his office. It will pay dividends.

Finally, remember that information drives *JUICE*. If you "forget", or withhold significant information from your lawyer, he will be acting with one hand tied behind his back. You certainly should try to avoid having your lawyer hear something for the first time from the company's counsel. That's not to your advantage and might well work to your disadvantage.

18.

Once You're In The Front Door

Contact has been made. Now it's time to try to negotiate a separation package that both you and your employer can live with. Assuming that you are going to conduct negotiations through a lawyer, the assertion of some type of legal claim on your behalf is implicit – often express. That is what distinguishes the *"Stick-Em Up"* approach from the *"Aw C'mon"* approach.

By now, your employer will likely have gone through at least a preliminary evaluation of its legal exposure. Often, this evaluative process was completed before the decision to terminate your employment was made. However, additional consultation by your employer with its human resource professionals, personnel specialists, your superiors as well as outside counsel will probably be undertaken in order to re-evaluate its position in the face of contact by your counsel and information presented by him.

Most employers will not seek to spend disproportionately large dollars in litigation with former employees where alternatives can reduce the exposure of such litigation and the associated costs. It's called risk management. Even where employers have purchased some type of employment practices liability insurance, the employer probably is responsible for paying substantial deductibles before the insurance kicks in. Dollars matter.

There are loosely three types of employer negotiating stances. Depending upon the type adopted by your employer, your negotiating strategy will necessarily vary.

There are those small employers who are confident in their actions and sure they have done nothing wrong. Then there are larger employers who likewise believe they have done nothing wrong and are willing to do battle over the issue. Finally, there are employers that do care about doing the right thing and make it a matter of corporate culture.

18.1. Type I: Small Employers That Are Sure That They Have Done Nothing Wrong

The first type of employer-negotiator is the small business that makes a decision to separate an employee based upon the owner or management's own, visceral business judgment – it's their business and they know what's best. This class of employer typically does not consult with counsel in advance, either because it does not occur to the employer that there may be legal issues which are relevant to its decision, or because employers of this size and financial position generally abhor paying lawyers. This class of employer may not even have a human resource or personnel function or staff with whom to consult.

For these employers, the potential for legal liability and exposure to monetary damages may be material to the company's overall financial health. As a result, such employers tend to be quite resistant to making substantial monetary payments to terminated employees in order to settle claims made by the employee. This class of employer has a deeply held view that it treats all of its employees dutifully, fairly and as family; that it goes out of its way to provide security, income and benefits for its employees; and that its decision to separate an employee is attributable to failings or deficiencies on the part of the employee or circumstances beyond the employer's control.

It is this class of employer that feels it has already done more than it should have done and thus is quite resistant to making any, let alone substantial severance payments. Of course, not every small employer falls within this category. If you are fortunate enough to have worked for a more paternalistic company, good for you. But on the small employer end of the spectrum, you should expect high levels of resistance from more employers than not.

Even if you were employed by this class of employer, however, you are not without *"JUICE"*. Nobody likes spending valuable resources on legal fees, but the prospect of spending big money by a small business (relative to its net worth, revenue or profit) can be a real game changer. The small business may not have the financial resources to fund a defense against your lawsuit regardless of whether it is completely blameless. That provides some leverage in the negotiations, albeit within fairly narrow settlement parameters.

If the small employer can spend some money to avoid the money pit of litigation and keep its business alive, it may grudgingly do so. But that likely means that only a modest amount of money will be available to pay you.

18.2. *Type II: Larger Employers That May Not Care*

The second type of employer is the larger company that makes a good faith effort to articulate comprehensive personnel policies and procedures and typically consults with its human resource staff and counsel before making a decision to separate an employee. To the extent this class of employer has been counseled about the termination action it is contemplating (or has taken), it is satisfied that the termination does not give rise to any legal concerns.

A caveat: sometimes an employer takes action even if it knows that doing so may be legally risky or questionable. However, even with the knowledge of the legal risks attendant to such a termination, this employer effects the termination anyway because it decides that its need/desire to separate the employee outweighs the risk of doing so. It decides to deal with the consequences if and when a claim if asserted.

It is possible, but less likely, that this type of employer received flawed legal advice. Or, even if not flawed, the advice may not be definitive because of the circumstances or unsettled legal nuances. Rarely is a case "open and shut". You always have to consider the possibility that a judge or jury will do the unexpected or simply see things differently.

Despite its size and resources to defend any claim you might bring, this type of employer may nevertheless want to bring absolute closure to its relationship with a separating employee by presenting the employee with a separation agreement at, or shortly after, notice of termination is given. After all is said and done, this class of employer, notwithstanding the advice that it has received concerning its legal position, seeks to look forward in terms of running its business and would rather not have to deal with a discontented former employee. Time devoted to addressing claims by ex-employees serves only to divert efforts and attention from its business activities.

Even where this class of employer has been advised that the actual merits of its legal position are strong, it may nevertheless decide to balance concerns about the appearance of its action (*i.e.* because of your race, age, sex, etc.). Under such circumstances, the employer with such concerns is more likely to seek to induce a separating employee to execute a release of all claims against the employer in exchange for the payment of some consideration, whether in the form of severance, salary continuation and/or benefits.

The manner in which the separation package is offered, as well as the amount of dollars offered in exchange for the release, may suggest the degree of sensitivity that the employer perceives may surround its termination decision. Your ability to reasonably evaluate your employer's position may substantially leverage your negotiating strength for an enhanced separation package – *JUICE.*

18.3. *Type III: Larger Employers That Do Care*

The third type of employer cares. It cares because it has established rules, regulations and procedures that are designed to ensure that employees are treated in a manner consistent with its corporate philosophy. It cares because its management team has been educated and trained to understand and follow these rules as consistently, fairly and non-discriminatorily as can be expected in a workforce riddled with subjective considerations. It cares when something falls through the cracks and its rules are not followed; or when the rules are broken; or when the system simply fails. And it cares if it believes that some inexplicable injustice (even one it is not willing to publicly acknowledge) has been done.

That does not mean that a decision to terminate your employment will be overturned. That is unlikely. It is far more likely that management will support whatever decision has been made, but attempt to ameliorate the consequences. Presumably, you have decided that even under these circumstances, the *"Aw C'mon"* approach will not bear adequate results and you have engaged counsel to negotiate with your employer on your behalf. In that context, an implicit threat of litigation may be enough to provide adequate cover for an enlightened, even if somewhat recalcitrant employer.

But note: just because your employer "cares", that does not mean that it will abandon sound business judgment and write a ridiculously large check to salve its corporate conscience. Rather, it may mean that a carefully crafted presentation by your counsel that articulates some of the concerns identified by him, along with a suggestion concerning his view of the strength of your legal position, may induce your employer to address some of these issues.

An employer in this class generally will not be bulldozed by your counsel. It will investigate the claims and issues raised by counsel and, where it believes that some wrong may have occurred, it will attempt to address these issues even if, at the same time, the employer denies any wrongdoing. Wild, frivolous claims without basis – either in law or in fact – do more harm than good in the negotiating process with this class of employer. These employers pride themselves as being enlightened and fair; a claim that smacks of "blackmail" will not be favorably received and will likely backfire.

19.

Getting Down To Negotiating

Most executives fancy themselves as skilled negotiators. While that may be true in the context of your day-to-day business activities, it may not be equally true when it comes to negotiating a separation package for yourself. In fact, traversing the process of separation and negotiating a comprehensive separation agreement requires a fair degree of distance, skill and experience.

You may receive little or no advanced notice of your termination from your employer. Often, when notice is given, a written 'package' may also be presented to you. The severance package that has been offered by your employer probably contains legally adequate consideration (something of value exchanged between the parties) to support your execution of a release in favor of your employer.

The reason your employer is offering this financial inducement is to "buy" the release and other commitments contained in the agreement from you and bring closure to its employment relationship with you. It also is trying to ensure that litigation does not follow. You should start with the assumption that virtually everything in the proposed package is negotiable to some extent. Time and process will tell how true that is.

This is not intended to be legal advice, *BUT*, unless there is a strong reason to do so, you should resist signing any document at the time it is presented to you by your employer. There may even be applicable legal requirements that you be given a period of time in which to evaluate the offer. For example, if you are 40 or more years old, you will likely be given either 21 or 45 days (depending upon the circumstances) to decide whether to accept the employer's offer. A period of reflection upon the events that have just transpired and time to consult with an attorney to review the document is appropriate. Likewise, you should be suspicious of a "limited time" offer which needs to be accepted on the spot or within a couple of days: it ignores the real world and may not be what it appears to be.

19.1. *Securing Sufficient Time Within Which To Consider Your Employer's Initial Offer*

Most severance offers carry some type of time deadline within which you are asked, or required, to respond by executing the document and returning it to your employer. While such a deadline should not be viewed as carved in stone, it likewise should not be ignored.

Start with the assumption that your employer's paramount interest is securing your signature on the separation document containing the release. Therefore, if you need additional time to have the document reviewed by an attorney or to consider various options and courses of action, you should not hesitate to make a request for an extension of time in which to decide whether to sign the agreement.

If you are going to make a request for an extension, it is preferable that you make the request prior to the deadline initially established for execution and return of the agreement. The request (or confirmation that an extension has been granted) should be made by e-mail or other method that will create a verifiable paper trail in case you need it later.

It would be somewhat unusual for an employer to refuse to grant additional time for you to review the separation agreement. Doing so only increases the likelihood that you won't sign the agreement and increases the risk that you will let the deadline pass and will pursue litigation against the company. Thus, most employers will accord you a reasonable amount of additional time to make sure that your execution of the agreement is knowing and voluntary and therefore enforceable.

Once you have retained counsel to deal directly with your employer, the decision as to whether to request an extension of time becomes less clear. To the extent that you personally request an extension of time in which to consult with a lawyer, such a request generally will not raise a red flag for your employer and will commonly be granted. That is all the more likely if your stated reason for the requested extension is because you have not yet found a lawyer to review the agreement or because the lawyer you want to consult cannot see you for several weeks.

However, your employer may reasonably draw a very different conclusion if your lawyer makes such a request on your behalf. In such circumstances, your employer may fairly conclude that the request is being made because you are unwilling to allow the time within which to execute the agreement to expire and therefore unwilling to risk having the offer withdrawn or lapse. That risk averse message could significantly undercut your *JUICE* and limit your negotiating leverage.

Thus, you should discuss with your attorney how to handle this issue. Will you let the date by which execution is required pass and assume the risk that the initial package will not be withdrawn? Or will you insist that your lawyer seek an extension of time in an attempt to reduce the downside risk? Or will you make the extension request on your own before your lawyer enters the picture and contacts your employer? Since there are several ways to handle this, you should make an affirmative decision how to proceed rather than deciding by default.

19.2. Ambivalent Negotiating Stance: Problems With "Testing The Waters"

Invariably, once a separating employee has been presented with a proposed separation package by his employer, he seems to be overcome by an irresistible urge to test the waters and see how much further the employer is prepared to go in terms of the salary continuance, severance and benefits than it has initially offered. This is a risky approach – it is effectively going down the *"Aw C'mon"* path and then reverting to *"Stick-Em Up"* which, as has already been discussed, is a bad idea.

"But isn't it a good idea to find out how far I can push my employer?" Sure, if it's part of a well thought through strategy. In fact, such a fishing expedition may well lead to a modification of the initial offer and result in an increase in severance and benefits. To the extent that you are prepared to accept whatever modifications, if any, result from such an approach, then the only remaining question is whether the separation document itself adequately reflects the understanding between you and your employer and adequately protects your rights and interests.

In that context, counsel's role is quite limited; review and analysis of the document itself without regard to the financial terms of the arrangement. *"Aw C'mon"* has worked for you.

However, unless you are fully prepared to live with the results of any approach you make on your own to your employer – including getting no additional severance – there are several problems with testing the waters.

First, it may be inconsistent with the concept of a well thought out business plan discussed above.

Second, and absent adequate time to reflect upon what is being offered against an evaluation of your legal rights by a lawyer, you have no way of balancing the value of the offered package against the value of any legal rights you may have. While this analysis is not necessarily dispositive of the outcome of negotiations, it plays an important role in evaluating your negotiating position, strategy and potential upside. Why ask for a bag of apples if you are entitled to a bushel? What if your employer grants your request for the bag? Now what? Can your attorney now go back and demand the bushel?

Third, you may make a request that signals your bottom line. To the extent that you are unsatisfied with your employer's response and then hire a lawyer to do battle with your employer (*"Stick-Em Up"*), your lawyer is now faced with negotiating with an employer that has already been told what you really want. While it is certainly possible for your lawyer to massage the outer limits of your previously articulated position, it is not easy to significantly revise your "ask". As a result, you may end up with only a marginal likelihood of overall success. The risks likely outweigh the benefits:

Employer to your lawyer:

"But, before you got involved, your client told me that he was disappointed with the Company's offer of 6 months of salary continuation and thought that 12 months was more appropriate. I offered your client 9 months just to get the deal done and now you're here demanding big money! What happened?"

Your lawyer to your employer:

"You should have done the deal when you had the chance; now that I have my hands on this case, it's going to cost you more."

OR

"My client was weak; once I got finished juicing him up, he now wants big money!"

OR

"My client didn't know what he was saying".... "My client was delusional"... "My client was just kidding."

It's certainly not impossible, but going down the *"Aw C'mon"* path first, and then hiring a lawyer to try the *"Stick-Em Up"* approach if you are not satisfied with the results of your own efforts, makes the lawyer's job significantly more difficult. In large measure, negotiating is about signals and messages. If you give mixed (let alone competing) signals, it may make drawing your employer out much more difficult.

Finally, there probably is a limit to the number of times that the human resource professional, or the lawyer or other individual representing your employer's interests in negotiations is able (or willing) to go back to the company's "financial well" on your behalf. After you have pushed once, twice or maybe even three times beyond your employer's initial offer, it becomes substantially more difficult for your lawyer to then enter the scene and dramatically enhance the package.

There are many manuals that give an in-depth treatment to various negotiating techniques and styles. Whether you have decided to negotiate on your own behalf or have retained an attorney with particular expertise in negotiating employment agreements, you need to devise a negotiating strategy. This is a two part process: define what you want and then decide how are you going to try and negotiate it.

19.3. *Strategy Relating To Contract Claims*

As we have already discussed, the law seeks to remedy breaches of contract by restoring you to the same position you would have been in had your employer not broken its agreement with you. In short hand, you can calculate the full value of what you were supposed to receive and then, subtract the amount that you actually received. The net amount (or the difference between full value of deal and what you actually received) marks the outer limits of your "contract damages".

Unless your agreement with your employer specifically provides for payment of your attorneys' fees, the law generally requires each party to bear its own legal costs in contract cases. Likewise, there generally is no right to punitive damages or an award for emotional suffering in contract cases.

Thus, the outer limits of your potential contract damages described above is just that; it represents your maximum potential recovery. Emphasis, however, on *maximum*. There are 2 reasons why that is the case.

First, negotiations are a process of give and take. That means that rarely does either party obtain 100% of its initial position. Second, the law requires those who have suffered from a breach of contract to make the effort to try and reduce the loss that the breach causes – it is called your duty to "mitigate" your loss.

In the employment realm, mitigation means that you have an obligation to seek other, comparable employment and to accept it where it is available. The amount representing the "*Outer Limits*" of your loss thus is reduced by what you earn during the period of the contract violation or by the amount that you could have earned during that period if you had exercised reasonable diligence in searching for new employment.

In sum, contract cases are only intended to make you "whole" – give you the benefit of your agreement – not provide you with a windfall as a penalty for your employer's breach. An overly simplified example based upon a valid breach of contract claim is described in § 16.1.

You should also remember that there likely is no right to contract damages after the term of the contract because you would have reverted to an at-will status on the day after the contract expired. As such, you would not be able to articulate a basis for damages from that point forward – you no longer had employment with a fixed term. Of course, if the contract provided for automatic renewal or contained any other provision which would create a contract *right* to a longer period of employment after the initial term, the assessment of contract damages might change. The result might also change where the applicable state law imputes an extension of the contract following its contract expiration.

It also should be noted that contracts often contain provisions that change the basic formulation of recoverable damages. For example, some contracts include a provision that specifies the amount of damages (or the manner in which they are to be computed) in the event of a breach. Some may eliminate the obligation to mitigate any potential loss.

The real message is as follows: the more senior you are; and the more experience and expertise that you have; and the more widely recognized your professional and business accomplishments; the larger the *Outer Limits* are likely to be; BUT the smaller the *Net Loss* is likely to be. While your stature may have provided you with a high value contract with theoretically large damages for breach, such status may also provide you with the ability to secure a comparable position in a reasonable period of time. The result may be a reduction in your *Net Loss* contract damages.

In the end, the name of the game in negotiations over contract claims is to beat the spread. While both sides can quantify the *Outer Limits* of potential damages in a contract case, neither you nor your employer may know your actual *Net Loss* at the time of the negotiations unless you have already secured a new job and the value of your mitigation can be determined. If you have a new job, you probably want to put negotiations on a fast track before your former employer finds out and discounts or reduces its settlement offer to account for your mitigation.

Resolving matters early, before the actual loss can be computed, provides an incentive to both you and your employer. It also carries some risk – but mostly to you – since your employer already knows its worst case scenario. Presumably, an early settlement will be for some percentage of the value of the *Outer Limits*. Otherwise, your employer has no financial incentive to settle at this point. If it will take full value (or something close to that), your employer has a low risk of testing your resolve to litigate. It can always settle for full value later and it still won't be responsible for your attorneys' fees.

Settlement gets your employer a release from you in exchange for payment of a fractional share of your potential (but, as yet, undetermined) contract damages. Conversely, you may be able to negotiate a package which turns out to exceed your ultimate *Net Loss* –you get compensation that exceeds your actual loss. That's a successful negotiation – potentially "win-win" on both sides.

19.4. Computing Damages If You Have A Viable Claim For Violation Of Your Statutory Rights

Damages in cases where there is a violation of a right created by statute are likely to be different from those available in a pure contract case. In most instances, the analysis above for computing damages attributable to your actual, direct loss of earnings is the same. The obligation to mitigate your loss generally is the same.

Differences in available damages between contract cases and cases involving violation of statutory rights are due to the fundamental difference in the way these rights were created. By and large, the law of contract interpretation and enforcement is judicially created, not legislated in statutory form. The rules have evolved in court decisions over the course of several hundred years going back to cases decided under British law to which some U.S. courts still refer.

While the law of contract cases is designed to make you whole – put you in the same position you would have been in had your employer not breached its agreement with you – cases involving violations of rights created by legislatures (U.S. Congress and state legislative bodies) may have additional goals. Some laws provide for damages for such injuries as pain and suffering, emotional trauma and distress; or provide for an award of front-pay (compensation for lost future earnings), punitive damages and attorneys' fees. Some statutes place limitations on the amount of damages that can awarded to you. This may vary from jurisdiction to jurisdiction and may depend upon the type of claim at issue. Finally, some cases are a hybrid containing both contract and statutory claims and damages are available for both such claims accordingly.

Properly evaluating the *Outer Limits* and *Net Loss* is critical in formulating your negotiating strategy. A lawyer who has extensive experience with an array of employment claims should be able to reasonably assess the *Outer*

Limits of damages that might be awarded to you as a successful litigant.

While the portion of damages attributable to lost back pay may be easily calculated, especially if you have found a new job in the interim, the other elements of damages such as emotional distress, punitive damages and attorneys' fees will be unknown. The difficulty in assessing the amount you likely will be awarded in damages for each such element is almost like trying to pick a winning ticket from a fishbowl while blindfolded. A jury might award $1 or $1,000,000 – and a Court might decide that the award is inappropriate and impose its own valuation. Your attorney may have spent a great deal of time preparing for, and prosecuting your case only to have a court decide that your employer should not be required to pay for all of those attorney hours for a variety of reasons.

Thus, damages in a statutory case impose an important unknown over the negotiating process in that neither you nor your employer can clearly quantify your respective upsides and downsides. The unknown provides an incentive for both sides to work toward a settlement. You are trying to avoid coming up short of expectations and your employer would prefer not to carry a contingent liability on its books or establish a sizeable reserve to pay any judgment you may get against it.

19.5. *The Value Of Settlement*

If you can successfully settle matters with your employer, you likely will settle for less than you really want or less than you think you are entitled to receive. Likewise, your employer likely will feel that it is paying more than it wants to pay and maybe more than it really can justify. Nevertheless, a relatively fast resolution of your claims has two potential consequences:

> ▶ First, it's possible that you may enjoy a financial "windfall" if you are able to settle with your employer quickly and lock in the financial terms of separation. That could easily happen if, for example, you are also able to quickly secure (or are close to securing) new employment. In that case, the value of the separation package you have negotiated may exceed your actual financial loss because your period of unemployment turns out to be shorter than the period represented by the separation package.

Thus, if you settle your claims for 6 months' of severance (even if you think you are entitled to more) but are unemployed for only 3 months, you have done well. That is because the damages formula would have compensated you for only the 3 months of unemployment. You would be 3 months ahead. Of course, the converse is true for your employer: had it not settled with you so quickly, it might have saved 3 months' severance after it found out that you were unemployed for only 3 months. Instead, it paid for 6 months when it might have gotten away with paying only for 3 months.

Hindsight is nice for both sides, except it changes the entire dynamics of negotiating a separation arrangement. The value of the unknown is part of the leverage that each party brings to the negotiating table.

> ► Second, and alternatively, you may take the 6 months' separation package but guess wrong, and end up being unemployed for more than 6 months. Assuming the strength of your claim and an inability to mitigate your damages, you may come up short. Good for your employer; not so good for you.

A negotiation is made successful by the ability of skilled participants to step into the shoes of the other party. The participants can fairly evaluate the needs of the other party. They can evaluate risk and try to accommodate the interests of all concerned. A negotiator who is blinded by the "rightness" of his position and who is unable to see things from the other side's perspective risks failure. While you do not have to agree with your employer's perspective, a successful negotiation requires that you allow for the possibility that you may be wrong or that your employer's contrary view is held in good faith.

19.6. *Prioritizing Your "Wish List" Items*

Prioritizing your negotiating demands will limit the risk of getting something you ask for, but do not really want. Discard those items that are clearly excess baggage.

Then reduce the list to those items that are truly important. Most employers that are willing to negotiate have a maximum dollar "pie" that they are prepared to spend to obtain your signature on the separation agreement and release. An employer may be willing to massage the pie somewhat, and it may also be willing to reallocate the dollars in its pie. The negotiations are the tool for maximizing the amount of the pie that you obtain.

Example:

>You have worked for XYZ Corp. for 10 years and your annual salary is $120,000. You get all of the usual benefits including employer paid health and hospitalization insurance; you anticipate being awarded a $60,000 bonus at year-end based upon company performance against set benchmarks; you have unvested stock option awards; you have a company car; you have been separated as of October 31st; and XYZ's written policy provides for 1 month of severance for each year of service and continued health and medical coverage for the severance period (10 months here). *Your Wish List:*
>
>Let's assume that you are **entitled** to $100,000 in severance under XYZ policy (1 month salary x 10 years of service) and continued health and medical coverage. (Note that the assumption is not valid if payment of severance under the policy is conditional –

i.e. you must first sign a release in order to qualify for the severance). Also assume that you want 18 months of severance instead of the 10 months under the policy, plus the $60,000 bonus, plus company paid health insurance during the entire 18 month severance period, plus accelerated vesting of your unvested stock options which will then give you 90 days after termination in which to exercise these options.

Analysis of your "wish list" vs. your employer's offer:

The additional severance you want (8 more months x $ 10,000) is worth:	$ 80,000
The bonus is worth:	$ 60,000
The additional health insurance is worth (assuming a $500/month premium):	$ 4,000
The stock is worth the spread between the exercise price and the highest price the stock will achieve before the option lapses.	?

Exclusive of the stock (which may not be an out-of-pocket expense for your employer) your wish list costs approximately $144,000 above your employer's standard policy. Suppose you ask for all 4 items. Now, suppose that your employer (i) agrees to pay for your health insurance until you get another job that provides you with health benefits (or agrees to such coverage up to a maximum period) and (ii) also agrees to accelerate your stock options. However, your employer rejects your request for 8 additional months of severance and also refuses to pay any bonus.

Your employer's agreement to provide 2 of the 4 items you requested looks like a 50% win. But it may be premature to congratulate yourself on getting half of what you asked for.

What if the options have a strike price that currently is "under water"? And what if the stock options expire before they are "in the money" – they never get to be worth anything before they expire?

What if you get a new job with health benefits within several months? If so, you negotiated a benefit with very limited value: you bought an expensive benefit but only enjoyed the premium cost of the health insurance for several months because you became covered by your new employer's benefit plan.

If you had focused your negotiations exclusively on cash, and had gotten NO additional severance but successfully negotiated payment of 10/12 of the $ 60,000 bonus (pro-rated because you worked through October 31st), you would have received an additional $50,000. You can pay for many months of health insurance premiums with that amount of cash; and you may only need to do so for a couple of months.

Thus, it generally does not make sense to buy a promise from your employer to pay for $4,000 worth of health benefits when you may only need $500 worth of that insurance. The remaining $3,500 provided you with no value and came directly out of the pie that your employer allocated to purchasing your release. Negotiations are not an open ended process grounded in the expectation that the more you talk, the more forthcoming your employer will be.

19.7. The Different Negotiating Stances

You should think through which type of negotiator you want to be and be sure to discuss this with your lawyer. Also consider whether the type of negotiator you "want" to be is also the same type of negotiator that you "can" be. You may want to win the boxing heavyweight championship, but recognize that doing so just isn't in the cards.

At the outset, you should map out your optimal position: what you consider winning the "gold ring". The much harder task is to then identify your bottom line. Doing so is a critically important part of developing your negotiating strategy – it may be the difference between significantly overshooting or undershooting your strategic goals.

Clients often worry that their lawyer is not going to be as aggressive a negotiator as the client wants. This causes some clients to hold back from disclosing their true bottom line position to their lawyer. The unspoken fear is that the lawyer will take the easy approach and steer negotiations toward the "bottom line" just to get a deal done and earn a fee rather than aggressively negotiating toward the client's optimal position.

Negotiating with your lawyer is a bad idea; and if you think you need to do so, you may want to change lawyers before you get too far into the process. Seasoned lawyers do not give clients short shrift; especially if the fee arrangement provides for significant upside to the lawyer.

19.8. The "Hard" Bottom Line

There are really two types of bottom lines - "hard" and "soft". A "hard" bottom line is a specifically defined, absolute, inviolate, non-negotiable bottom line:

"I want X and I will not take less than Y."

"Y" is a specific amount, benefit or other, identifiable item or combination of cash and benefits. "Y" may have been derived by formula, your understanding of your employer's prior treatment of other employees, your estimate of your expenses until your find a new job, or pure emotion. You may not even be sure how you arrived at that number, but you are sure of one thing – you won't take any less. In any event, "Y" is fixed and identifiable – for example, you want 12 months of severance ('X') and will not settle for anything less than 6 months ('Y'). Your negotiator's job is to get you as close to "X" as possible – *or, alternatively* – as far away from "Y" as can be achieved.

A specifically defined, "hard" bottom line makes your negotiator's life easier. That's because it requires skill to keep pushing your employer closer to its bottom line (which, of course, you will not know) without crossing it and losing everything. A "hard" bottom line – by definition – means that you have decided to reject even $1.00 less than the number you have staked out as your bottom line.

As a result, a "hard" bottom line reduces the negotiator's risk of making a mistake by pushing too hard. The worst that can happen is that you could have had $99 but lost it all because you told your lawyer that your "absolute", "inviolate", "bottom, bottom" line was $100. Unless that is true, it is not a bottom line and all you did was negotiate with your lawyer and ended up on the losing end.

Example:

Your "gold ring" (your "X") is $250 and your "bottom line" (your "Y") is $100. Your employer's initial offer was $50. After the first round of negotiations, you reduce your demand to $200 and your employer raises its offer to $75. After the second round, your demand is reduced to $150 and your employer raises its offer to $85. After the third round, you again reduce your demand to $125 and your employer responds by making its final offer of $97.

Now What?

Your lawyer is a savvy negotiator. He understands that "bottom line" means "bottom line". So, he pushes ahead in the face of your employer's final offer and makes a last, best offer of $100 on your behalf to your employer.

Oops – now your lawyer gets a letter from your employer withdrawing its final offer and says that it will see you in court.

Your lawyer, being pretty pleased with himself, advises you that there will be no settlement and you should march straight to the courthouse door and file suit immediately.

Once your head stops spinning, you ask your lawyer the proverbial question? *WHAT HAPPENED?*

The answer is simple: either (i) the parties could not close the $3 actual gap between their respective bottom lines and you are disappointed, but not unhappy that your lawyer was not able to squeeze water out of the stone because $100 really was your bottom line; OR (ii) you were negotiating with your lawyer, or changed your mind – in either event, you really did not have a fixed, bottom line, and now regret that you could have closed the deal at $97, but instead have nothing but litigation to look forward to. Had your lawyer known your true desire, the negotiations might have ended differently.

19.9. *The "Soft" Bottom Line*

That brings us to the second, more fluid, "soft" approach to negotiations – a "bottom line with an attitude." This approach looks at a bottom line as a point of real resistance, but not necessarily a drop dead number. As a result, your negotiator must be careful not to risk the $97 even when your resistance point is $100. You might be unhappy about it, but, after all is said and done, you will accept the $97 offer rather than litigate.

If you think that you have a bottom line, ask yourself whether an offer of $1 less than your declared bottom line will result in instructions to your lawyer to start a lawsuit. If so, stick with it; if not, make sure your negotiator understands the program.

The reason that an early determination of your negotiator status with your attorney is important is because there is a nuanced difference in the language used between the "hard" and "soft" bottom line approaches. And language is all important in negotiations.

For example, the language of the "hard", fixed bottom line may be any one of the following:

"No."

"The proposal is rejected."

"Are you authorized to accept service of legal papers?"

"No deal."

"Negotiations are over."

"We'll see you in court."

In contrast, the language of the "soft", fluid bottom line necessarily is more tempered, as follows:

"I don't know if I can sell that to my client."

"I don't think that's in the cards."

"That's beyond the scope of my authority."

"I'm having trouble seeing how we are going to close the gap between us."

The former leaves no wiggle room while the latter leaves the door open just enough to re-visit the last conversation between negotiators.

19.10. *Diagrammatic Examples of "Bottom Line"*

Regardless of the good faith efforts and best intentions of the parties, a negotiation can only be successfully concluded if there is some common ground between the parties. If not, the dispute cannot be resolved. The negotiators role is to try to find that common ground and extract the fullest concession from the other side to its advantage. The following geometric concepts illustrate this point:

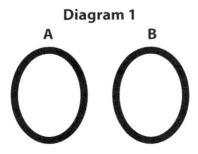

Diagram 1

If both your optimal goal and your bottom line fall somewhere within circle A, and your employer's top and bottom number fall within circle B, there can be no settlement. The diagram makes it clear that there is no common ground between you and your employer's positions. There is not even the slimmest of territory where the amount that you will accept matches the amount that your employer is willing to give.

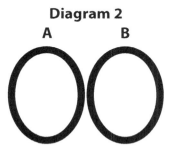

Diagram 2

In Diagram 2, the positions of the parties have tightened and there is less gap between the outer limit bottom line of the parties, but there is still no common ground and therefore no deal is possible.

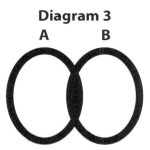

Diagram 3

In Diagram 3, the shaded area represents common ground. As narrow as it is, it represents an area where agreement can be reached. The art of the negotiation is finding the outer limits of that area that most serves your interests. Because the shaded area is so slim, there is significant risk that either party can overplay its hand and cause the process to fail.

Diagram 4
A B

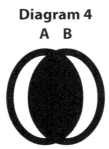

In Diagram 4, the shaded area also represents common ground. Here, however, there is significant overlap of positions as reflected by the larger shaded area. This provides room for aggressive negotiations since there is room to push without necessarily overplaying your hand. Unlike Diagram 3 where the shaded area is so narrow that agreement may elude the parties, negotiations in the context of Diagram 4 should more easily result in agreement. Your negotiator's job is to push the negotiations as far to the outer limits of your own circle as possible; your employer will attempt to keep you as close to the center as possible.

Part Four

Done Deal . . . .Almost

Part IV addresses the technical aspects of closing the deal – negotiating the language of the document. Even where the basic terms of the document (*i.e.* the company's standard separation agreement) are reasonably acceptable to you, it is important that you pay attention to those provisions of the agreement that may have significance as you move on. While the preferred approach is to leave discussion of the language in the agreement until after there is agreement on the financial terms, there is some risk in doing so.

For example, where you resolve the financial terms before addressing the language, your employer may properly view language as secondary to you and assume that it can impose its will in that regard. From your employer's perspective, language may be the *quid pro quo* for the money. And now that the money is within your grasp, your employer may evidence very little, if any, flexibility over the language of the agreement. From a pure leverage analysis, it's hard to fault your employer's view that if it satisfies most of your financial demands, you are unlikely to walk away from the entire package because of language issues.

On the other hand, raising language issues before there is agreement over financial terms increases the risk that you telegraph to the employer issues which are of high concern to you. Your employer may "smell" the opportunity to force you into making concessions in your financial demands in exchange for concessions in language that you want (*i.e.* relief from a non-compete). You may also transmit your willingness to accept the ultimate financial terms – why else would you be negotiating language at this point?

20.

The Separation Agreement

At some point – either at, or subsequent to the time your employer notifies you of its decision to terminate your employment – you may be presented with some type of written separation agreement containing the offered separation package. Depending upon the tone your employer wants to convey, along with the legal advice it has received, the separation document can take the form of an informal memorandum, a letter that you are required to countersign as an acknowledgment of your acceptance, or a more formal document denominated as an 'agreement' (*e.g.* "Separation Agreement"; "Settlement Agreement"; "Confidential Agreement and General Release"...).

The somewhat schizophrenic employer feigns the softer approach by tendering a letter ("Dear Sue"), but trips over itself by crafting a single spaced letter which sometimes runs 6, 8 or 10 pages long in barely understandable legalese.

20.1. *What Am I Missing: Agreement Basics*

Employers generally do not present separation packages that are intended to 'snooker' you by making promises that they do not intend to keep. Rather, any difficulty in enforcing promised benefits generally comes later when there is confusion or disagreement about what was promised and/or intervening circumstances that the employer claims relieves it of its obligation to make good on the promise (*i.e.* violation by you of a post-employment restriction or obligation).

Indeed, the most common events that give rise to resistance or refusal on the part of an employer to fulfill the promises made by it in a separation agreement, occur where:

- ▶ the employer believes that you are competing or soliciting employees or customers in a manner, or during a time period, when you agreed you would not do so; or

- ▶ a new manager becomes responsible for overseeing administration and compliance with the agreement and was not party to the negotiations leading up to the agreement and has no loyalty to the deal; or

- ▶ your employer does not believe that you are making a good faith effort to secure alternate employment and has agreed to pay severance only if you do so and only while you are unemployed; or

- ▶ the company's financial position takes a dramatic turn d o w n w a r d and the company is looking for an excuse and way to save money.

Regardless of the form of the separation document, all variations are intended to memorialize the terms of separation between you and your employer with a view toward eliminating litigation arising out of the separation. The common thread through the various types of agreements is a document that should clearly establishes the following:

- when the separation occurs;

- the nature of the separation (voluntary, involuntary, retirement, by mutual agreement, etc.);

- the status of accrued compensation and benefits;

- who/what is agreeing to do what and for whom;

- the date on which each undertaking or promise is to be accomplished or satisfied;

- the particulars of what is being provided by you and your employer to the other; and

- a recitation of the "what-if" consequences that attach in the event either party fails or refuses to carry out their end of the deal.

Most agreements contain additional provisions such as a release, confidentiality, non-disclosure and an agreement not to sue that are intended to ensure closure of the relationship.

Language in the agreement that deals with non-financial matters generally does not stand in the way of closing a deal. The exception is where a provision at issue is one of high institutional concern to your employer such as a confidentiality undertaking, or a restriction on competition or solicitation of employees or customers. In fact, it is more likely that language in the agreement will be a "deal breaker" for your employer than it will be for you. However, where there is an issue of significance to you, you and your attorney should be sure to carefully strategize how and when you will deal with language relating to that issue.

20.2. General Rules To Guide Your Negotiations

There are several good rules to follow when reviewing, and then negotiating acceptable language in the separation agreement.

First Rule: *The Rule Of "15"*

It is very important that the final agreement be clear on all points. Depending upon the complexity of the separation arrangements, the negotiation and drafting of the settlement agreement may involve a number of professionals representing you or your employer including lawyers, financial advisors, accountants, and executive compensation, benefits, retirement and tax experts.

Clarity in the agreement is important because it should reduce potential disputes and misunderstandings about what the parties intended. As a general proposition, ambiguity favors the employer because it is the paying party with the deeper pockets. That enables the employer to leverage disclarity of interpretation of ambiguous language in its favor.

A good test of the document's clarity is to give the final draft of the agreement to a reasonably bright 15 year old high school student. If that student can tell you what and how much you are supposed to get; when you are supposed to get it; what, if anything, can intervene to cause you not to get it; and what you are agreeing to do (or not do) in return, the document passes the threshold test of clarity – the *Rule of 15*.

But unless the document is clear enough for a 15 year old to answer those questions with specificity, the document is not clear enough for you to sign.

The rule? The separation agreement should be clear, easy to understand and unambiguous. Otherwise, you may end up in litigation with your employer over either its, or your unsatisfied expectations.

Second Rule: Who Owns The Ambiguity

As a general rule of contract interpretation, ambiguity in contract language is construed against the party that drafted the language. The reason is that the drafter had the wherewithal to draft clearly; if it fails to do so, it bears the responsibility.

As a result, it is not uncommon for agreements to contain a provision that states that both parties bear equal responsibility for the drafting of the agreement – whether that's true or not. By doing so, the intent is that neither party is held responsible for any ambiguity.

The rule? Draft language you are prepared to "own".

Third Rule: The *Zipper* Clause

The *'zipper'* clause is discussed in greater detail below. This provision is almost mandatory in an agreement. In short, the provision says that you have no right to anything that is not specifically addressed in the agreement. That is not to say that a verbal promise made by your employer (but which is not included in the written agreement) will not be honored – but it does mean that you likely will have no legal right to enforce that promise.

The rule? Make sure everything that you expect to receive or to happen is specifically addressed in the agreement. Leaving something out is the surest route to unmet expectations.

Fourth Rule: 'It's Not Worth The Paper It Is Written On'

Most contracts, – even the most carefully prepared documents including separation agreements – tend to induce a false sense of security on the part of the separating employee. Having hired a lawyer and having thoroughly reviewed and revised the separation agreement (it now satisfies the *Rule of 15)* you view the signed agreement as solid as a cashier's check: *the agreement says so, therefore it must be so!*

Employment contracts and separation agreements are supposed to be enforceable road maps of the rights, obligations and responsibilities of each party to the other. It will not come as a shock to any seasoned executive that contracts sometimes are not entirely honored and sometimes they are completely ignored – either actively or passively.

As is true with contracts generally, neither employment nor separation agreements are 'self-enforcing'. That means that regardless of how clear an agreement is – no matter how clear and unambiguous your rights are under the agreement – and no matter how unconditional your rights may be, neither you nor your lawyer has the capacity to "force" your former employer to honor the commitments it made to you under the agreement. Only a court of law has that power. And that means that you may automatically be in a lose-lose position because of the cost of obtaining enforcement of your rights even where there is no doubt that you have been wronged. The cost and risk of pursuing your rightful due can make the value of the chase diminish rapidly.

As was discussed above, each party is responsible for bearing its own attorney's fees in contract cases, unless the contract specifically provides to the contrary. The separation agree is such a contract.

The rule? Try and negotiate a provision in the agreement that your employer will pay your attorney's fees if you have to pursue it for breach of the agreement.

Fifth Rule: Boilerplate

It should not be necessary for a seasoned employment lawyer to start from scratch and recreate contract language to address standard issues in a separation agreement. Counsel should have easy access to provisions addressing these same issues as part of an office form file or database culled from agreements the lawyer or his firm have previously drafted. There is nothing unprofessional about using time tested language. Indeed, where boilerplate language serves as a starting point for crafting final language, it can save time, effort and money.

But every provision, whether "boilerplate" or newly crafted language, must be tested against the result the language seeks to achieve. Boilerplate can be a ticking bomb if a provision is simply "cut and pasted" without being tailored to the nuances of your situation. Language that has already been tested in court and has survived a challenge to its legality or enforceability is obviously most valuable. Familiarity with the nuances of these provisions and how they tend to fare in court makes the lawyer with expertise in this area worth his weight in gold.

The rule? Make sure you work with a lawyer who has experience with separation agreements rather than someone who is doing your agreement as his first. It's not like every other type of contract.

Sixth Rule: Is It An Enforceable Contract?

Whether the document is denominated as an "Agreement", "Release Agreement", "Separation Agreement" or other euphemism, the document that you will be signing, after it has been satisfactorily negotiated, is intended to be an enforceable contract.

A basic underpinning of contract law is that the promises in the contract must be supported by "consideration" in order to be enforceable. In loose terms, that means that the party making the promise is suffering some type of legally recognized detriment: it is agreeing to do something which it is not otherwise obligated to do (*e.g.* pay money) or, conversely, agreeing not to do something which it has the legal right to do (*e.g.* work for a competitor). It is the exchange of the promise for the consideration provided by the other party that creates the binding nature of the agreement.

Thus, it is important to evaluate whether you are entitled to the compensation and benefits offered by your employer in the proposed separation package under your state law, or under an employment contract or some other agreement that you had or have with your employer. Applicable corporate policies and longstanding company practice should be examined.

If your employer is already unconditionally obligated to do something for you, then its agreement to do so will not suffice as consideration for the promises being made by you in the agreement. As noted above, your employer suffers no legal detriment if it extracts a promise from you in exchange for receiving something that you already have a right to receive. Additional consideration, above what you are already entitled to receive, is required in order to make your promise enforceable. The reverse also is true.

Example:

> Your employer wants you to agree not to sue the company for anything that happened during your employment or arising out of the termination of your employment. In order for your agreement not to sue to

be enforceable, your employer must provide you with some type of consideration in exchange for your promise (*i.e.* you agree not to do something you have a right to do in exchange for something given to you by your employer that it does not have to provide).

Now, suppose that your employer has a severance policy that unconditionally provides for 1 month's salary for each full year that you have worked for the company, but only if your employment is terminated by the company for any reason other than 'cause'. If you have 6 years of service as of the date of termination, you would be entitled to 6 months of severance. That's nice, but alone, payment of that amount is not sufficient to support a promise by you not to sue. That's because you are entitled to the 6 months of severance even if you refuse to promise that you will not to sue. Additional consideration from your employer is required to make your promise legally enforceable.

If however, your employer agrees to pay you 7, 8, 9 months or any amount of severance in excess of your 6 month entitlement, there will be adequate consideration and your agreement not to sue should be enforceable.

Of course, it is an entirely different ballgame if the company's severance policy specifically requires that you must sign a separation agreement in order to receive the severance. In that case, your right to the 6 months of severance is conditional – you get the severance only if you sign an agreement (which will contain your agreement not to sue).

The package being offered by your employer (including subsequent modifications) should be evaluated against this backdrop. It certainly is possible that the severance offer made by your employer is generous because you have been a good team player and you are well liked within the organization.

It also is possible that you are entitled to some or all of the compensation and benefits offered in the package regardless of whether you sign the agreement. Thus, the marginal portion of the offer – that portion which is above and beyond your *entitlement* – is the only true consideration that you should weigh against the value of the promises you are being asked to make.

The key issue, of course, is whether you are entitled to the payment or benefit without signing the agreement. If you are an at-will employee, virtually everything accorded to you as an employee can be viewed under the law as a gratuity. Your employer, as the provider of the benefit/gratuity, can generally establish whatever eligibility and qualifying standards for benefit entitlement that it likes. However, and depending upon how each such benefit was created, the gratuity may morph into an enforceable right.

Thus, there probably is no difference between the enforceability of two severance plans, one of which unconditionally promises a fixed amount of severance per year of service and a second, which makes the same promise contingent upon the departing employee signing a release in favor of the employer. Both may be legally enforceable, although the latter has a conditional requirement (*i.e.* signing a release) attached as a predicate to receipt of the severance.

The rule? Be sure you are getting something of value in exchange for the promises you make in a separation agreement. In the example above, consider whether you are willing to make the promises required by your employer in exchange for any additional severance offered to you that is above the severance to which you are already entitled.

• • •

The separation agreement will probably address a wide range of issues depending upon the complexity of the arrangement. Not all provisions discussed in the following chapter are relevant or applicable to all circumstances. Provisions that may be relevant to your situation should each be discussed with your attorney prior to finalizing any separation agreement. Additional, special provisions dealing with circumstances unique to your situation may also be appropriate.

21.

***Getting Started:
General Rules Of Contract Interpretation***

Before moving into a discussion of specific provisions that commonly are found in a separation agreement, a word about how contracts are interpreted by courts is useful. The discussion is equally important when drafting an employment agreement when you get your next position. Clear and unambiguous contract language should be the goal. Your employer may not comply with the requirements of the contract, but, at least, its obligations will be clear. If that happens, and you cannot resolve the matter informally, your only effective remedy is to file a lawsuit against your former employer that asks the court to enforce your contractual rights and compel your former employer to perform its contractual obligations.

21.1. *The Role Of The Judge In Deciding Your Lawsuit*

Once you file your lawsuit, the court that will decide whether you are right will have your legal papers, including the contract at issue, in front of it. The court also will have legal papers presented by your former employer explaining why it did not breach any contractual obligation to you. Its defense may turn on your post-termination conduct that your employer claims relieved it of its obligation to perform the "clear and unambiguous" provision.
Alternatively (or along with its other arguments), your employer may claim that there is a genuine dispute as to

the meaning of the provision. It will be difficult to carry the day in court with that argument if, in fact, the provision is "clear and unambiguous". But imagine if instead, the provision is indeed ambiguous and susceptible to different meanings – which could make the difference between winning or losing your lawsuit.

Thus, careful contract drafting and attention to each clause is crucial to a successful and litigation free transaction. Having said that, even the best drafted contract can result in litigation. But the best way to limit unmet expectations that result in litigation because it turns out that you and your former employer were not both "on the same page", is to pay attention to detail in every clause of the contract, including the so called "boiler-plate" language. You should never allow superfluous clauses to remain in the final contract.

Regardless of the outcome, resolution of your dispute in court may turn out to be an unsatisfying experience. Consider the time that is involved with legal proceedings and the costs of the litigation which you will have to pay yourself unless the agreement in dispute has a specific provision that shifts the cost burden to your former employer. Moreover, remember that a judge (who is only human) is trying to figure out what a contract means and is doing so in hindsight, perhaps years after the agreement was drafted, and maybe after some of the key drafters are no longer available.

The court's job is to read the contract and decide what it means and, based upon its interpretation, determine whether your rights have been violated. It is not a court's role, nor does it have the power to impose contract terms on the parties. A judge really is trying to figure out what obligations the parties imposed upon themselves. In order to fulfill that function, courts have developed a variety of rules that judges use to guide them through the process of contract interpretation.

These rules have evolved based upon judicial experience and are designed to determine the real intentions of the contracting parties. Since judges are not mind readers when they try to identify the parties' intent, and all kinds of things may have changed or happened since the agreement was finalized, judges sometimes get it wrong. As a result, the less you need to reply upon a judge figuring out what your agreement means, the less likely you are to end up in litigation or, if you do, the more predictable the likely outcome.

Some of the more common rules applied by the courts are discussed below. These rules generally are matters of state law so that one state may apply a rule that another does not or two states may apply the same rule differently. Moreover, some states have additional rules that may be relevant as well as statutory provisions that may apply.

21.2. *The Overriding "Main Purpose" Rule*

The Main Purpose Rule provides that when interpreting the meaning of an agreement, the primary intent and purpose of the parties must prevail and the court may not re-write the agreement. To arrive at the primary intent and purpose, plain words will be given their plain meaning, while technical terms or words of art will be given their technical meaning. Unless otherwise indicated, all parts of the contract will be construed together; doing so often will disclose the intent from the document in its entirety which it is necessary to construe those parts of the contract which are at issue or ambiguously worded.

A contract will be read as a whole and every part will be interpreted with reference to the whole document and in such a way as to give effect to the main purpose of the agreement. When the contract contains preprinted, typed and handwritten words which are arguably conflicting or ambiguous; preference generally will be given in the following order: (1) handwritten, (2) typed, and then (3) preprinted words.

21.3. The Plain Meaning Rule

The Plain Meaning (or "Four Corners") Rule provides that if the agreement or the specific contract term in question appears to be plain and unambiguous on its face, its meaning will be determined from the four corners of the document without resort to extrinsic evidence.

21.4. Lawful, Effective and Reasonable Interpretations Are Preferred

Consistent with the rule providing that all parts of a contract should be given effect where possible, an interpretation which renders the contract lawful, effective, and reasonable is preferred over interpretations which render the contract unlawful, invalid, or impossible to perform.

Moreover, courts favor a construction of a contract which will uphold a contract rather than defeat it. Where two constructions are possible, one of which will defeat a contract, the other uphold it, the latter construction will be adopted.

21.5. Taking Circumstances Existing At Contract Formation Into Account

In order to interpret the main purpose and primary intent of the parties, a court may take into account the circumstance existing at the time and place of its execution.

21.6. Ambiguities Are Construed Against The Drafting Party

Essentially this rule provides that where two different meanings can equally well be ascribed to certain words in a contract, the meaning to be adopted is the one that is least favorable to the party that drafted the offending words. The rationale for this rule is the assumption that it is within the power of the drafter of the contract to employ words that make the meaning clear, and if the drafter failed to do so, he should not profit by his negligence.

Thus you should expect to see a provision in the separation agreement that says (even if not true) that the agreement was drafted by both you and your employer and that any ambiguity will be deemed the result of the drafting by both parties. That is intended to protect your former employer from the general rule of construction which holds that any uncertainty in a contract will be construed against the drafter – which almost always is the employer.

21.7. "Usage Of Trade"

The words of a contract generally are to be understood in their ordinary and popular sense unless the parties use them in a technical sense or a special meaning is given to them by usage (*i.e.* technical words in a contract will be interpreted as usually understood by persons in the profession or business to which they relate, unless clearly used in a different sense). A contract is interpreted according to business custom and use in the place where it was made or will be performed. This rule recognizes that in a particular business, certain words may have a different or trade meaning that all members of the group recognize and use.

Where a custom or usage is shown to be generally adopted and known, the words will be considered as having been used in the sense such custom or usage attaches to them. Likewise, if a custom or usage is shown to be of such general and well-known nature that the parties must be considered (in the absence of contrary evidence) to have acted in reference to it, such custom or usage will govern the meaning of the terms used.

21.8. *Omitted Terms*

What happens when the parties omit an essential term from their contract? Generally, the court will supply a term which is reasonable.

21.9. The Parol Evidence Rule

Where the parties have reduced their agreement to final written form, evidence of prior or contemporaneous agreements (verbal or written) will not be relied upon by a court to vary or contradict the terms of the final written agreement. The parol evidence rule provides that if the court finds the writing to have been intended as a complete and exclusive statement of the terms of the parties' agreement, then the writing alone constitutes the contract and evidence of prior negotiations or "side agreements" will not be used in interpreting the final written agreement.

• • •

These are just some of the more common rules – there are many more. Knowledge of at least the existence of these rules is important so that you appreciate how important it is to spend time on the agreement after terms have been agreed upon, and to get it right. It is your best protection against having unmet expectations later on.

22.

Non-Financial Terms Of Settlement

Each separation agreement is a composite of financial and non-financial terms. Your natural tendency will be to gloss over the non-financial language once you have reached agreement concerning the financial terms. Your lawyer should serve as your brake. As rewarding as it is to get the severance, you don't want to be penny wise and pound foolish. Language may be more important to your employer, but there are minefields in contract language that can create long term difficulties for you. Proceed expeditiously, but judiciously.

Take the time to get it right.

22.1. The Parties

As basic as it sounds, every agreement should contain a specific recitation of the parties to the agreement. Most often, the employer should be defined as your actual employing entity and likely will include the parents, subsidiaries, divisions, affiliates of that entity and all of the officers, employees, directors and related individuals of each of those entities. Careful identification of the employer is of particular importance where all payments to you are not made simultaneously with execution of the agreement and you need to rely upon the long-term financial vitality and existence of the entity that is supposed to make later payments. Issues of subsequent business bankruptcy, sale of business and shell corporations are obviously important in defining the responsible entity and the obligations that attach to each specific entity.

Likewise, "you" should be defined to include your heirs, successors, assigns and your estate as beneficiaries under the agreement in order to ensure that even if you die prior to receipt of all payments due to you under the agreement, the payments will be made to your survivors.

22.2. The Nature Of Separation

Many separating employees and, sometimes employers, insist upon a provision in an agreement acknowledging that the termination is really a resignation; or is by "mutual agreement"; or is due to a reduction in force; or the result of a corporate reorganization. There is probably an inverse relationship between the importance of how the separation is characterized and your status in the corporate hierarchy. Thus, the more senior you are, the less important the characterization of termination is likely to be.

If you want to characterize your separation as a "voluntary resignation" or separation "by mutual agreement", ask yourself why. For starters (and this goes back to prioritizing your wish list), if you want your employer to agree to such a characterization, your employer may extract a price from the settlement pie for its agreement. In addition, and depending upon how senior you were, a prospective employer probably will have access to your superiors to determine the exact nature of your separation. Indeed, newspaper or other news reports of related events often create a paper trail with which you have to deal. The characterization in the agreement may be of little value.

Particularly in circumstances involving less senior employees, prospective employers will likely find it hard to believe that you voluntarily walked away from your job and income stream "to pursue other opportunities" – before you landed a new position, particularly in times of a tough economy and tight job market.

Thus, be cautious about buying something in the agreement which, again, is of little or no value. Indeed, where resignation is the proffered reason for separation, it may well raise the specter of a hidden or unarticulated cause that might raise other concerns on the part of a prospective employer.

Nevertheless, there may be specific reasons to characterize a separation one way or another. One such consideration involves circumstances where there is an underlying legal obligation to accurately report or disclose the reason for, or circumstances surrounding your separation. For example, certain Wall Street and other financial institution employers that are licensed by various regulatory bodies (*e.g.* FINRA) are required to report the fact of, and reasons for certain separations to these bodies. With respect to employees of financial institutions, this frequently is accomplished with the filing of a U-5 form (unique to the securities industry) that identifies and categorizes the separation. Financial industry employers should not, and generally will not misrepresent in a U-5 filing.

Moreover, there is developing state case law that involves a duty of a former employer to disclose certain known traits about an employee to inquiring prospective employers. For example, suppose an employee is found to have engaged in grand larceny of his employer's property, or serious sexual assault upon a fellow employee. In an attempt to avoid the embarrassment that a public hearing of these charges might cause, the employer accepts the employee's immediate resignation and the injured co-worker refuses to press charges. Subsequently, a request for a reference arrives from the departed employee's prospective employer. Wham! What does the former employer do? Express profound regret at the employee's decision to resign? Risk subjecting a new employer (and its employees) to a known risk without disclosing same?

The lesson is that circumstances often dictate the required outcome even where the participants to the negotiations may be of a contrary, common view. Thus, if there is an issue of concern pertaining to your departure, your ability to spin the characterization in the agreement may be limited and of limited value. That may be true even though most employers generally will respond to requests for references only by confirming dates of employment and perhaps some limited additional information. Moreover, employers are reluctant to agree to one characterization in the separation agreement and a different characterization to a third party.

A second consideration involves the consequence that a specific termination may have with respect to your entitlement to certain benefits. This is one area where language may straddle both financial and non-financial issues. An example of one such benefit is your entitlement to unemployment insurance benefits. State law will govern this right although federal law may provide additional benefits.

Generally, your entitlement to unemployment benefits will be contingent upon your loss of employment through no fault of your own. That means that a resignation without a good reason likely is as disqualifying as is a termination for "cause" or misconduct. Since severance will not last forever, you should balance the value of a "resignation" against the potential loss of unemployment benefits because of such characterization if you are still unemployed when the severance runs out.

Another example of a potential financial impact may be equity grants or awards *(e.g. stock, options, etc.)* that you received at the time of your hire or during the course of your employment. Some such awards or equity plans may have provisions that cause a forfeiture of unvested equity or the cancellation of option exercise rights depending upon the circumstances surrounding the separation. You should review each equity award and plan document to determine the consequences that flow from the various termination events. It is possible that you have significantly different rights under these plans if you retire, or your employment is involuntarily terminated without cause than if you resign or are terminated for cause.

Finally, rights under health insurance, disability and related benefit plans should be examined in order to determine whether there are any issues relevant to benefit eligibility that are dependent upon characterization of the termination.

22.3. *The Date Of Termination*

Both your last date of work as well as your last date of employment should be specified in the agreement. They are not necessarily the same. The last date of work will be easy to determine because it probably is the day that you stop going to work. The last date of employment, however, may depend upon what the agreement says, as well as any applicable employer personnel policies, rules and regulations. Each of these dates may be negotiable and may be important in terms of when post-separation benefits begin. They are also relevant to your status during the period between your last day of work and your last day of employment if they are not the same.

It is conventional wisdom that it is easier to secure new employment while you are still 'employed' than it is when you are among the ranks of the unemployed. As a result, an issue which is often the subject of extensive negotiation is whether you will be retained on your employer's payroll for a period of time following your last day of work (*i.e.* through the date of termination) and the nature of your status during the intervening period of time. This may be critically important in terms of how you are able to hold yourself out to prospective employers. "I used to be employed by/worked for" versus "I am currently employed by . . . ." It is important to be sure that your employer will provide information that is consistent with what you tell prospective employers.

The dates may also be important in terms of vesting rights or accrual of benefits that are tied to your age, years of service or active service status with your employer. These considerations generally relate to such benefits as pension rights and vesting and other rights under various equity awards. Each plan, award, grant and program document should be carefully reviewed to determine whether there are critical dates which trigger rights or benefits. A careful examination should be made in this regard where a termination date is December 30, or 31, or just before the end of calendar or fiscal quarter, or the final day of the employer's fiscal year.

Example:

> Your employment is terminated on December (or June) 30th. Had you still been employed on January (or July) 1st – one day later – you would have vested in a significant number of stock awards that are otherwise subject to forfeiture under the terms of the equity plan because you were not on the payroll on that magical date.

> Or

> On December 30th, you were 54 years old (plus 7 months) – just 5 months shy of a generous early retirement program including retiree health benefits, etc. for which you would have been eligible had you still been employed on your 55th birthday.

The mere confluence of the timing of your termination and your loss of benefits is not dispositive. But such timing may be strongly suggestive that your employer's motivation for terminating your employment on a specific date was improper – timed in order to deprive you of your vesting or other benefit rights. That, in turn, may supply added *JUICE* in negotiations with your employer.

Finally, the termination date may unintentionally create a conflict between your status as an employee for purposes of salary continuation and your obligations to any new employer.

Example:

> Suppose you have been employed by XYZ Corp. as Vice-President of Marketing for 5 years and have been separated as part of a company-wide reduction in force. Skillful negotiations have yielded a separation arrangement to keep you on XYZ's payroll as an employee for six months and XYZ has agreed to pay your salary and continue to provide your benefits during this six month period. Salary continuation is an important consideration under XYZ's benefit plans to ensure your continued eligibility to participate in these plans. With the wind at your back, you quickly secure new employment as Manager of Marketing for a competitor. There is nothing in your agreement that specifically restricts such employment.

The problem with continuing as an 'employee' of XYZ Corp. comes into sharp focus when you are simultaneously supposed to be an employee of your new employer. Even where there is a knowing consent to your dual employment by both employers (which would be unusual in itself), you still should avoid being on the payroll of two employers at the same time. There is a minefield of potential concerns that relate to such issues as confidentiality, conflicts of interest, and use of non-public competitive information along with the an inherent conflict between the duties of loyalty and fidelity that you owe an employer if you are trying to serve two masters at the same time.

By way of example, what happens if you are assigned duties by your new employer that are directed at and designed to place your former employer (on whose payroll you remain) at a competitive disadvantage? Or consider whether your former or current employer owns, or has a legal or proprietary right to any "invention", "discovery" or "creation" you may make while you are simultaneously employed by it and by another entity. Clearly, you do not want to litigate these issues and, if XYZ Corp. is not happy about your new position, that may be the result.

One way to protect against these types of conflicts and potential disputes is for the separation agreement to provide that you will give notice to your separating employer of the date on which your new employment will commence. It also should provide that your employment with the separating employer will end on the day immediately preceding your first day with your new employer. That ensures that there is no overlap of dates on which you are an employee who is simultaneously on the payroll of 2 separate employers. It also ensures that you can adjust the start date with your new employer to protect any vesting or other benefit rights that may be date sensitive.

In addition, once you give your separating employer notice of your new job, the separation agreement ideally should provide for either (i) the acceleration and lump sum payment to you of all remaining unpaid salary continuation payments; or (ii) continued payment of the remaining amount due to you over a defined period, but as severance rather than salary continuation.

Finally, and to the extent that you will continue with the separating employer in some employee category, the separation agreement should clearly define what, if any, continuing duties or responsibilities you will owe to that employer. Will you be required to work any minimum hours per week? Will you be required to be 'on-call'? Will you be required to report to the office? It is important that you know exactly what, if anything, that employer expects from you during the period of salary continuation so that you avoid a dispute as to whether you are performing as expected.

22.4. *The Release*

The single most important provision in the agreement – at least to your employer – is the release. While the form and content of releases vary from state to state, the essence of the release provision is the finality that it brings to the relationship.

Generally speaking, the release closes the door on your relationship with your employer. The release is usually the longest provision in the agreement. By entering into an agreement with a broad release, you agree to walk away from whatever legal rights (whether or not you know that you have them) that you had, might have had, might have, or could have against your employer. The language of the release is retrospective: it is effective from moment you sign the document looking back in history. Some releases use the words "from the beginning of time . . ." to say the same thing. But the release stops when you sign it; anything that occurs after you sign the release, such as a defamatory reference, is not released and remains actionable.

The release is a complex legal contract. It relieves the released party or parties from all kinds of general and specific historical conduct. Most often, the conduct that is released is described in broad-based, sweeping and unlimited terms, intending to cover anything and everything that a room of lawyers could draft. A release generally is not limited in time or geographic scope and is applicable even to conduct that neither you nor your employer know about.

The intent behind the release is to provide your employer with closure to its employment relationship with you and obtain a high level of confidence that it will not hear from you again – no claims, no lawsuits, no complaints. That's what it is buying. Accordingly, unless there are specific rights that you should carve out and exclude from the scope of the release, your employer is entitled to the broadest release it can draft. And while the parties can agree upon various exceptions, exclusions, carve-outs, and limitations, every such exception leaves the beneficiary of the release (generally the employer) exposed because the releasing party (generally the employee) has left the door open to pursue the released party for the excluded conduct. It may be highly unlikely to happen, but an open door is an open door.

22.4.1. *Mutual Or Unilateral?*

Releases can be unilateral or mutual which means that either you alone release your employer or it releases you as well. It is, of course, preferable to extract a release from your employer so that you are confident of closure in both directions of the relationship. However, the more senior you are, and the larger the company, the more difficult it is to negotiate an unconditional, complete release in your favor from your employer.

Generally, the corporate party line is that the employer cannot give you a release because it has no way of knowing everything that you might have done during your employment. Or whether you have engaged in any conduct (active or passive) that could result in a lawsuit, loss, claim or governmental investigation. Another common refrain (although not really any different), is the employer's argument that its obligations to its shareholders do not allow it to provide you with a release.

These arguments have some merit, but also are somewhat circular. On the one hand, the company is prepared to pay you a significant sum of money on your way out of the company while, on the other hand, it wants to reserve the right to pursue you should it later decide that you have engaged in some type of actionable wrongdoing. Potential claims that might be raised against you based upon your personal conduct, such as sexual harassment or misconduct or financial improprieties are not easily forgiven by an employer.

Obtaining a release from your employer may also depend upon the type of industry in which you were employed. Some industries present a low risk of unknown employee wrongdoing, while others, such as the financial services industry, are rife with risk. Many investment bankers, brokers and other brokerage firm and financial institution employees effectively are freelance employees risking sizable amounts of their employer's (and customer's) capital. Sometime the results of their activities remain unknown or undetected until well after employment has terminated.

Assuming that you have nothing to hide, one way to induce your employer to provide a release in your favor is to propose language incorporating an affirmative representation by you that you have not done anything that could cause loss to the company:

Example:

> "You represent to Employer that, up to the date of execution by you of this Agreement, you have engaged in no conduct not already disclosed by you to Employer, or which could have been discovered by Employer through the exercise of ordinary business diligence, which could cause Employer to suffer a material financial loss. On the basis thereof, Employer forever releases. . ."

In that way, your employer can reasonably rely upon the fact that you have nothing to hide because if your representation turns out to be false, the company may be able to pursue you for a breach of contract. While this is less than ideal (*i.e.* the door has not been firmly closed), it may be the best you can obtain. A caveat: you should do some serious soul-searching and be sure to have a candid conversation with your attorney if you believe that there may be an issue lurking in the background that could come back to haunt you. That is especially true if you are giving consideration to proposing the foregoing representation. If so, you will need to make a calculated business and legal judgment as to the risk of saying nothing and praying that the issue never matures or dealing with it at that time.

As an alternative, and still better than nothing but not ideal, is a representation by your employer to you that, as of the date of its execution of the separation agreement, it does not know of any state of facts that could give rise to a claim against you.

> "Employer represents to Employee that, as of its execution of this agreement, it is not aware of any state of facts that could give rise to any type of claim by Employer against Employee."

Moreover, if the separation agreement provides you with defense and indemnification (*see* discussion below), or requires your personal assistance so that your employer can defend itself in a matter in which you were involved, you may decide that the risk of obtaining something less than a full release from your employer tips in your favor.

In the final analysis, however, remember that you are probably not better off without any severance deal at all because you stood your ground by insisting upon a mutual release that your employer would not provide, than you would be with a separation agreement that did not contain a release in your favor. In both cases you do not have a release. And, in the former case, you not only do not have a release, you also do not have the financial and other benefits of the separation package! In the latter, at least you have the cash.

22.4.2. Release vs. Termination Of Obligations

When it comes to an employment contract you had (or currently have) with your employer, note that there is an important difference between being released from claims that you or your employer may have against the other *under* the employment contract and the termination of the contract itself.

Example:

> At the outset of your employment, you entered into an employment contract with your employer that contained, among other provisions, a confidentiality and non-disclosure promise along with restrictions on certain of your post-employment activities such as working for a competitor and soliciting your employer's employees. Stock options granted to you during the term of your employment likewise contain similar restrictions. Assume that your employment is terminated without cause prior to the expiration of your employment agreement. After protracted negotiations, you strike a deal with your employer that is memorialized in the form of a separation agreement and which contains mutual, broad based releases by you and your employer in favor of the other.

Discussion:

A properly drafted release should eliminate any liability that you may have for any prior conduct including any past breach of the provisions of the employment agreement. But the release does not necessarily also terminate the employment contract itself which means that your post-employment obligations to comply with such non-disclosure, non-competition and non-solicitation provisions will survive and continue to bind you.

As a result, and if it is important to be relieved of such post-termination restrictions, you should be sure that the separation agreement (either in the release or elsewhere in the agreement) separately, and explicitly, terminates the employment contract **and** extinguishes all obligations that could survive termination of employment. Such a provision should also apply to company policies that may govern certain of your post-employment activities even in the absence of an employment contract:

Example:

"Employee and Employer agree and acknowledge that any and all prior contracts, arrangements, deals, agreements and understandings by or between them, whether written or verbal, and whether formal or informal, and all undertakings, obligations, promises, obligations and responsibilities under each and all such agreements are hereby canceled and terminated with no provision thereof surviving execution of this separation agreement."

22.4.3. Exceptions, Exclusions & Carve-Outs To The Release

You should consider adding certain carve-outs (exclusions) to the release that you provide to your employer. While benefits such as vested pension and qualified 401k benefits likely are protected by federal law and generally are not subject to forfeiture as the result of the termination of your employment, there may be other plans or programs in which you were a participant that create an issue.

If you want to preserve rights under such plans or programs, you should seek to incorporate a representation by your employer into the separation agreement as to each of the specific plans and benefits in which you were a participant and a particularization of your rights/benefits in each. Employers often are resistant to making such a representation because they are afraid of being wrong. However, most employers will at least confirm that "whatever you had, will be preserved":

Example:

"Notwithstanding any other provision in this Agreement and/or the Release given by you to the contrary, nothing in this Agreement or Release is intended to waive or release any rights and benefit entitlements that you may otherwise have arising out of your participation, if any, in any employee benefit, pension, retirement, deferred compensation, savings and investment or 401(k) plan(s) [etc.] .... maintained by Employer during the term of your employment."

If you have reason to be concerned that a potential claim against you arising out of your employment (such as a claim of sexual harassment by a former co-worker or subordinate) may exist, you should try to secure carve-out language that provides you with some ability to defend yourself (also see next section about indemnification and defense) in the event any such claim is made after you enter into the separation agreement with your employer.

Even if you are not aware of any specific circumstance that might give rise to a claim against you, it still would be prudent to try and obtain this type of carve-out. It probably is unlikely to happen, but you should avoid having your hands tied behind your back. Here's why: the term "company", "firm", "employer" (or whatever other term is used in the agreement to mean your employer) is usually defined in the separation agreement to include not only your actual "employer", but all of the company's former, current and even future employees of business units and entities you may never have heard of. There could be thousands or hundreds of thousands of people covered by the release.

That means that the release that you are giving your employer in the separation agreement protects all of these known and unknown individuals and entities from being sued by you. But even if you are getting a mutual release from your employer in your favor, most of the people and business entities that you are releasing will not also be releasing you – your employer cannot agree to release you on their behalf. You could only be protected if each such individual or entity signed the release - - which is not going to happen.

As a result, and even though it is unlikely to happen, you should consider whether to ask for language that protects you from being blindsided by a claim against you from any such person. The following carve-out language will provide a nominally level playing field in the event of such a claim:

> "In the event any person who is an intended beneficiary of the foregoing release, but not a signatory to this Agreement, shall institute, file, commence, prosecute and/or assert any claim, charge, legal action or proceeding against you, alone or with others, then, and in such event, the said release herein as it relates to such person and/or entity shall immediately be and remain forever null and void as if never given and without regard to any statute of limitations."

What this means is that the release from you in favor of your "employer" will release everyone that your employer wants you to release including all of those individuals you never knew. Most of the individuals who are the beneficiary of your release probably will never know about it. But the foregoing language protects you by providing that if someone who was supposed to be released by you (except for the company) decides to sue you, your release of that person is no longer valid – you can sue them back assuming you have a basis for doing so. The trigger in the provision is wholly within the control of the third party – if they leave you alone, they cannot be pursued by you. However, if they chose to assert a claim against you, that person loses the right to hide behind your release.

Example:

Suppose a co-worker has accused you of sexual harassment. Your employer, XYZ Company, investigated the claim but was unable to corroborate the accusation. In fact, the allegation was not true and made up by a disgruntled co-worker. Following the alleged incident, the co-worker has made the same allegation to other XYZ employees as well as key players in your industry.

Sometime later, and unrelated to the co-worker's claim, your employment with XYZ terminates and you are presented with a separation document containing a broad based general release. You sign the separation agreement and the release, which, because of its breadth, covers and includes this co-worker – not by name, but as part of the "current and former employees" category.

You start looking for a job. For the first time, you hear about your co-worker's actions. You now understand why you are having such difficulty finding a new job in your very small industry. It's like you have become radioactive.

Compounding your troubles, the co-worker now files a sexual harassment lawsuit against you. You want to react in the strongest way and sue the co-worker right back for defamation.

Uh oh! How are you going to feel when you find out that you can't sue the co-worker for defamation because you released the co-worker when you signed the separation agreement and the defamatory comments pre-dated the release. It's probably not worth expending a lot of capital to pursue such language unless there is a concern that you might be faced with a claim. Moreover, a carve-out from the release that preserves your right to defense and indemnification may provide adequate protection and is discussed below in the next section.

22.5. *Indemnification & Defense*

Defense and indemnification are two separate, but closely related concepts. This is an important provision: it may be the difference between draining your financial resources so that you can defend yourself against a claim arising out of your employment and having the protection that your former employer or some other third party (*e.g.* an insurance company) will stand behind you and absorb the costs of defense on your behalf.

Depending upon your status within the corporate hierarchy, you may be protected by statute, or may have rights that are contained in the company's certificate of incorporation, its corporate by-laws, insurance policies or some other vehicle that provides for defense and/or indemnification in the event you are sued for a covered act that is alleged to have occurred during your employment. This is a complex area and should be carefully reviewed by you with your attorney – particularly if you are a senior executive or have reason to believe you are at risk of a claim being made against you.

22.5.1. *Defense*

An agreement to provide you with a defense against a claim that has been made against you involves an undertaking by your employer either to provide you with a lawyer it selects at its cost, or to pay for a lawyer who you hire to defend you. But there are many nuances that should be considered.

For example:

- ▶ What if there is an actual or perceived conflict of interest in the event you and your employer are represented by the same attorney?

- ▶ Do you have the right to insist on separate counsel to be paid by your employer?

- ▶ If you are permitted to retain your own attorney, will the company pay your lawyer's bills on an ongoing basis?

- ▶ Or will you be reimbursed for your legal fees only after you pay the bills?

- ▶ Or will you be reimbursed only at the end of the litigation?

- ▶ Is there a cap or limit on the amount of legal fees for which you will be reimbursed?

- ▶ Will you be reimbursed only if you win?

- ▶ How is 'winning' defined?

- ▶ Do you need to prevail on all claims; or only a majority of claims, etc.?

Clarity and definition are very important in this area – the costs of defense can mount very quickly and be quite high. *See Rule of 15.*

22.5.2. *Indemnification*

Indemnification involves your employer's promise to assume responsibility for and pay any monetary liability that may ultimately be assessed against you based upon your alleged conduct – assuming that the law allows the company to do so in connection with the specific claim at issue.

The types of claims which are most often asserted against employees involve claims by shareholders, customers and clients dissatisfied with management or with company "results", and claims alleging individual acts of wrongdoing by you such as sexual harassment, discrimination or financial improprieties involving the company.

A release, even if you have obtained one from your employer, will not shield you from claims made by individuals or entities who/which are not parties to the release. Remember, the fact that your employer has agreed not to sue you does not limit the rights of a shareholder, client, customer or other company employee to do so.

Some jobs carry a higher risk of potential claim against you than others. This is particularly true for senior executives of publicly traded companies. If your job – or your conduct – has exposed you to potential claims, a provision for your defense and indemnification by your employer in the separation agreement is quite important. Possible provisions range from: (xx) a broad provision by which your employer agrees to provide you with counsel and/or defense at the company's cost along with its agreement to pay any judgments or awards against you; to (yy) a provision that defers a decision as to whether to provide you with any such protection to a later date depending upon the nature of the claim, the circumstances and outcome. Of course, there are many possible variations of rights in between.

The latter (yy) effectively translates into a reservation by your former employer of a right to decide how important you will be to the company's defense before deciding how forthcoming it will be in terms of your defense and indemnification. As a result, these issues obviously are better addressed now, rather than later, when you may have less leverage.

Generally, there is some middle ground that you can negotiate. For example, your employer should not object to a provision in the separation agreement that provides you with the same protection and coverage for defense and indemnification that you had while you were employed. That's not bad, but you might want to investigate the scope of that coverage. If you had no such rights while you were employed, such a provision will accord no such rights if you need them later.

The best protection is a blanket agreement to cover you:

Example:

> "Provided, however and notwithstanding anything else to the contrary in this Agreement or the Release given by Employee in favor of Employer in this Agreement, Employer agrees that it will defend and indemnify Employee against any legal action, proceeding, claim or charge, action and/or proceeding (collectively referred to as a "Claim") made against Employee, individually and/or with others."

Since it is unlikely that your employer will provide you with greater rights than you had as an employee, the next best approach is to ensure that you have no less rights:

Example:

> "Provided, however and notwithstanding anything else to the contrary in this Agreement or the Release given by Employee in favor of Employer in this Agreement, Employer agrees that it will defend and indemnify Employee against any legal action, proceeding, claim or charge, action and/or proceeding (collectively referred to as a "Claim") made against Employee, individually and/or with others, to the same and fullest extent that Employee would have been entitled to be defended and/or indemnified under any federal or state law, rule, regulation, statute, or under any Company by-law, policy, practice, rule, regulation or applicable insurance policy(s) in effect and/or applicable to the period during which Employee were employed by Employer and/or the date on which each such Claim is made or asserted, whichever provides Employee with the greatest coverage and protection."

22.6. Non-Competition And Other Restrictive Covenants

Employers can be schizophrenic. They have no problem jettisoning a "non-productive", "disappointing performer" while, at the same time, they also insist that this same employee agree not to work for a competitor. In one fell swoop, you may go from "worst employee of the month" to the greatest threat to your employer's competitive position.

The more senior you are, and the more technically and competitively sensitive your position, the more likely it is that your employer will seek some type of limitation on your post-separation activities. You may have already agreed to such post-employment restrictions in documents you signed when you first started working for the company or at various times thereafter.

There are 4 basic categories of post-employment restrictions discussed below that employers traditionally try to impose. The first such limitation is a prohibition against the solicitation by you of your employer's current employees, recently departed employees, employees who leave shortly after you, consultants and other service providers.

Second, is a prohibition against your solicitation of business from, or the performance of work for your employer's clients, accounts, customers and related 'assets'.

Third, is a prohibition against the disclosure of information that is designated by your employer as confidential or proprietary.

Fourth, is a limitation on your ability to work for, provide services to, or otherwise associate with another business entity that competes, in whole or in part, with the 'business' of your employer – perhaps even including parts of the business with which you had no involvement.

Books have been written and there are volumes of cases deconstructing each of these issues. Each potential restriction raises sophisticated legal concerns. As a result, any language proposed by your employer should be carefully reviewed – word by word – with your lawyer. Presumably, the lawyer you have engaged has expertise in these matters and can parse the nuances of each such provision and advise you concerning the enforceability of the provision under applicable law. But counsel is not a mind-reader. You should be sure your lawyer fully appreciates your current plans, potential plans and even remotely possible plans for the future. Benign sounding language that you rush through in order to get the deal done can come back to haunt you later. *See Rule of 15.*

Thus, even if you are confident that you will not re-enter the workforce in a manner that would run afoul of these restrictions, you should exercise extreme prudence by ensuring that your options are preserved. If you cannot negotiate such flexibility now, you likely will find it harder to do so if the actual need arises. By then, you probably will have even less, if any, leverage.

This is particularly important where monies are to be paid to you by your employer over time and where payment is contingent upon your compliance with the promises you made in the separation agreement. The cost of asking for relief from a restriction in the separation agreement may be high. The *quid pro quo* may be foregoing unpaid compensation in exchange for relief from a post-employment restriction.

22.6.1. *No-Solicitation Of Employees*

No solicitation provisions run the gamut from a legitimate effort by an employer to protect a reasonable business interest, to the absurd. Depending upon the language used in the separation agreement, certain restrictions may be permissible and pass legal muster – assuming they pass the preliminary "laugh out loud funny" test which is a base line test applied by some judges. You probably do not want to be involved in litigation over these issues. There is both the cost to you of such litigation as well as the risk that your new employer may get involuntarily enmeshed in such a litigation. Not a great way to start with a new company.

Unless your new employer is unique, it will want you to honor your commitment not to solicit and will want you to protect it from the consequences of litigation over your conduct. Likewise, you also should be careful about being perceived as someone who does not honor contractual obligations – it's not the best way to start a new employment relationship. As a practical matter, engaging in prohibited conduct – even if you have been advised that the restriction is unenforceable – can only increase the risk that you will be called to account for your conduct. Moreover, if you guess wrong and it turns out that your conduct was on the wrong side of the line, you may forfeit remaining severance payments, be assessed money damages and place your new employment at risk.

If you are leaving employment with a Fortune 500 (or other large) company and have agreed not to solicit employees, the language of the non-solicitation provision raises a number of drafting concerns. Preliminarily, the defined scope of individuals to whom the restriction applies should be carefully reviewed. This issue involves two subsidiary matters.

The first relates to identification of the scope of individuals who are prohibited from engaging in the solicitation.

For example, the restriction could apply only to you: "You may not". Or it may encompass others who are not identified by name: "You may not 'directly or indirectly.'" "Indirectly" is used in an effort to be sure that you cannot use someone else to engage in solicitation that you cannot do yourself. Thus, if you have agreed not to solicit a specific individual or class of individuals for 6 months following your separation, you probably cannot provide a manager, or the personnel office at your new place of business, with a list of prospects to enable them to 'cold-call' these individuals themselves. That includes a verbal as well as written list.

The second relates to the universe of employees that you have agreed not to solicit. From your employer's perspective, the broader this group, the better. If this type of solicitation has any relevance to you, you should be sure that the universe of individuals to whom it applies is narrowly defined.

Presumably, the term "employer" has been defined somewhere in the separation agreement. As discussed in §22.1, this definition likely includes your actual employer, and its parents, subsidiaries, divisions, affiliates, successor and assigns – and all of their past, current and future officers, directors, employees, and agents. You cannot possibly know the identity of all such entities and individuals – especially those who have not yet been hired. As a result, prudence dictates that you try to narrow the definition so that you and a third party can readily determine whether your proposed conduct will cross the line – *Rule of 15*. A restriction that prohibits your solicitation of employees of your "employer" simply is overly broad.

Finally, be sure that there is a defined time frame: does the restriction apply to employees employed by your former employer at any time while you were employed; or to employees who were employed as of the last date of your employment; or to individuals who left their employment with your former employer during a defined period? An example of the latter: "you may not solicit anyone who was employed by the company at any time during the 6 month period preceding your termination." This type of language is intended to protect your employer from your solicitation of one or more employees who resign prior to, and in anticipation of your departure so that you could claim that these individuals fall outside of the universe to which the no-solicitation applies.

Thus, even when you fully intend to comply with your promises, overly broad language may cause you to unwittingly run afoul of your promise in the event that you solicit someone who you did not know was covered. One way to limit this risk is to attach a list of all covered entities and individuals to the separation agreement. This may be only marginally helpful and somewhat unwieldy – and will likely be unacceptable to your employer. Alternatively, you can try to limit your no-solicitation obligation to only those employees you supervised, or those who reported to you, or those who work in your business unit.

It may be appropriate to specifically exclude individuals you brought with you when you first joined the company such as your assistant or secretary.

If you intend, or want to reserve the right to solicit employees of your former employer, be sure that the language in the separation agreement clearly demarks the line between permissible and prohibited conduct. Fuzzy language will not be your friend. *Rule of 15.* You would not be the first clever ex-employee to try to devise a creative method for hiring a former colleague and claiming that you did not run afoul of a no-solicitation restriction.

But a judge won't easily be fooled into believing that a former colleague just happened to read a newspaper advertisement placed by your new firm recruiting for an individual with skills, background and experience only that person possesses – and a circulation only in the village in which the prospect lives! Or that you did not "solicit" – rather, your former colleague sought you out and begged for a job. It might happen that way, but carefully crafted language is the best protection.

22.6.2. No-Solicitation – Customers And Accounts

Courts generally view restrictions on a separating employee's right to solicit an employer's customer or accounts favorably where the employer can demonstrate that it has an identifiable, legitimate business interest and need to enforce such a restriction. However, it is difficult for an employer to establish such an interest if the company is selling a product to customers who can readily be identified by a search of the internet or through the purchase of 'lead' lists. Under such circumstances, there is nothing unique about the employer's relationship with the customer – anyone can access the customer information with a little bit of ingenuity. Thus, there is nothing for your former employer to legitimately protect because you do not have to use any information developed by and belonging to your employer in order to solicit for business.

However, where your employer can establish that it has expended significant sums developing a customer base and where it is difficult to identify potential customers without using non-public information concerning its customers' product preferences, pricing and purchase history obtained solely through your employment, your employer has a much better argument and likelihood of success.

As a result, language in a separation agreement restricting your right to solicit customers and accounts should be carefully drafted to identify the customers (by name or class) to which the restriction applies.

- ▶ Does it apply to all of your employer's (remember to review the scope of the definition of "employer") customers?

- ▶ Or does it apply only to those customers in your business unit?

- ▶ Or just to those customers with which you had some contact in connection with your job during a defined period (*i.e.* within the 12 period prior to your termination date)?

- ▶ Are customers with whom you had a relationship prior to your employment excluded?

- Are customers you brought with you to your employer excluded?

- How broad is the restriction?

- Are you restricted from soliciting the customer?

- Or from doing business with the customer?

- Or from performing services for the customer?

- Or from having any contact with the customer?

In sum, the restriction should be defined so that the proscribed conduct is clear, and the customers that are covered can be clearly identified along with the time period during which the restriction will apply. *See Rule of 15.*

A note of caution: even in the absence of an explicit restriction or prohibition on solicitation, you are still not entitled to act with absolute freedom and impunity. Judicially created "common law" imposes independent restrictions on your conduct. Thus, for example, even if you do not have an employment contract or separation agreement, or if you have such an agreement it does not say so, you may not solicit or induce a customer to break a contract it has with your employer in order to switch its business to your new employer or for any other reason.

Nor are you entitled to solicit the customer utilizing non-public, proprietary information that belongs to your former employer.

22.7. The Non-Competition Provision–General Considerations

The third type of post-employment restriction is the traditional notion of a restrictive covenant – a limitation on your employment or business activities following your separation. These provisions commonly are referred to as "non-competes". There is an obvious opportunity cost that comes from removing yourself from the job market for any period of time. The direct costs are such things as loss of income and benefits; the indirect may include the non-economic costs involved with re-entering the marketplace after a hiatus, explaining your absence from the workforce during the intervening period, and adjusting to, or obtaining re-training for any intervening technical or industry related developments.

The courts of most states are openly hostile to outright prohibitions on an individual's right to work and are not overly hospitable to restrictions that fail to satisfy a basic business necessity test. These tests vary from state-to-state and your lawyer should be able to guide you as to the enforceability of proposed provisions in your state.

Inasmuch as the enforceability of a non-competition provision generally is a matter of state law, a provision in your separation agreement specifying the state law that applies ("choice of law") may be very important. That's because the same, or a similar contract provision, may receive quite different treatment and interpretation depending upon the state in which enforcement of the contract provision is sought. The result also may vary depending upon the court reviewing the matter; the competency of counsel on both sides; the culture of the employer; and the nature of the job market.

Much as you would like your lawyer to predict with confidence how a court will rule in these cases, your lawyer probably will not be able to do so (and probably should avoid trying to do so just to satisfy you or get you to sign on as a client). Guesstimates as to likelihood of success or outcome is as much as you can expect from your lawyer – and you may not even get that much. Don't ask your lawyer for percentage chances that you will "win". This isn't Las Vegas – and even there, a 99% chance of winning is small comfort to the 1% that lose.

Some non-competition provisions are clearly problematic or unenforceable under the law that applies. With respect to such provisions, your counsel may advise you that the proposed non-competition provision in the separation agreement that has been drafted by your employer will be difficult for your employer to enforce. The lawyer may even give an opinion that the specific language in the draft under consideration is likely to be outright unenforceable. Your lawyer's implication may be that you should not worry about making the promise not to 'compete' because the provision will likely not be enforceable if the matter should get to a court of law. Not so fast.

While your lawyer's legal analysis may turn out to be accurate, it also may ignore a critical consideration. The ultimate legal determination of enforceability generally can only be made by a court of law. But remember, once the issue of enforceability of a promise you made gets in front of a judge, you most likely are playing defense because you are being sued by your former employer based upon your alleged breach of the non-competition provision.

Often, an employer's efforts to enforce a restrictive covenant will start with an application to a court seeking an injunction prohibiting its former employee from continuing to engage (or starting to engage) in the objectionable conduct (*i.e.* going to work for a particular company). Depending upon the court to which the application is made, and local court practice, this type of restraint may be fairly easy to obtain. Indeed, final adjudication of your rights may take quite some time and during this time you may be under a total or partial injunctive restraint and unable to work while the legal case is pending and progressing.

Accordingly, it may not matter at some point whether a court of law will ultimately hold that the non-competition provision at issue is unenforceable. In real life terms, you may not be able to afford the time, cost and the risk of the litigation involved to get to a final court determination.

Unfortunately, your former employer can cause you all kinds of expense and loss of work even when it seeks to enforce a highly questionable non-competition provision. The larger the employer, the deeper its financial pockets. Those deep pockets make the cost of litigation against you less of a consideration for your employer than it probably is to you. As a result, the analysis of a non-competition provision needs to take into account both your lawyer's view as to the ultimate enforceability of the provision as a matter of law, but also the risk that you face in fighting that battle – regardless of whether you ultimately win or lose in court.

When deciding the issue of enforceability, most courts will look to the type of conduct that the contractual prohibition seeks to limit, along with the business rationale and need for the restriction, the "consideration" underlying the restriction, and the geographic scope and the time period to which the restriction applies. The more specific the business interest that an employer can identify, and the more closely tailored the geographic and time limitations are to that identifiable interest, the greater the likelihood that the provision will be enforced.

Examples:

> Suppose that you are a used car salesperson. It is unlikely that a court would enforce a "non-compete" that prohibits you from working as a used car salesperson anywhere in the United States. While the used car employer at which you worked might have some conceivable argument that you should not be permitted to work at another used car lot right next door for a short period of time (and even that might be a difficult argument), it is hard to see any legitimate business interest that your former employer could identify that would justify keeping you out of the used car sales force in the next town, state or across the country.

Now, suppose that you are a scientist working for a bio-tech company and have been a key player on a team of scientists that has recently discovered a cure for cancer. It may be easier for that employer to argue that it has a legitimate business interest in prohibiting you from working in cancer research and development for another bio-tech company for 6 months following your separation.

Some employers (particularly in the financial services industry) attempt to impose a "time out" on employees who want to leave their firm and join another employer or other financial industry employer. These firms try to do so by requiring a departing employee to give the firm notice of their intent to resign (generally 60 – 90 days). The firm then directs the employee to stay home during this 60 day notice period, effectively keeping the employee out of the industry – and out of contact for this 60 day period during which the employee remains employed by the firm. Employees who are placed on such "garden leave" generally continue to receive their normal pay during the notice period and continue to be covered by any contractual obligations, at least until their notice period expires.

22.7.1. The Non-Competition Provision – The Impact of Termination on Enforceability

There is some trend that indicates that courts are reluctant to enforce non-competition agreements in cases in which the employer terminates an employee without cause as contrasted with situations in which the employee resigns. Some of these courts will examine whether the termination by the employer was done in good or bad faith. If done in good faith, some of these courts may not consider the termination as a factor weighing against enforcement. On the other hand, if the termination evidences bad faith on the part of the employer, courts are increasingly resistant to enforcing the otherwise enforceable non-competition agreement.

22.7.2. The Non-Competition Provision – The "Employee Choice Doctrine"

Courts sometimes try to ameliorate the impact of a non-competition provision by imposing their own judicially created rules. An example of one such rule is the "employee choice doctrine". This rule has specific applicability where the employer makes the employee's right to receive post-employment benefits contingent upon the employee's agreement to and compliance with a non-compete agreement. Example: a stock option plan or deferred compensation plan provides for the forfeiture of benefits if the employee voluntarily leaves to work for a competitor.

The reason that this practice is permitted is because the doctrine rests on the premise that if the employee is given the choice of either preserving his rights under his contract by refraining from competition or risking forfeiture of such rights by competing, there is no unreasonable restraint upon the employee's liberty to earn a living.

The rule assumes that the employee makes an informed choice between forfeiting his benefit or retaining the benefit by avoiding competitive employment. Moreover, under the employee choice doctrine, if an employee leaves his employer voluntarily, the restrictive covenant at issue generally will be enforceable regardless of its reasonableness– the employer gets enforcement and the employee gets the benefits.

Conversely, it has been held that an essential element of the employee choice doctrine is the employer's willingness to continue to employ the employee. Thus, where the employer terminates the employment relationship without cause, the employer's action is viewed as destroying the mutuality of obligation on which the covenant rests as well as the employer's ability to impose a forfeiture. As a result, if an employee is terminated involuntarily and without cause and then competes with his former employer, a court will generally not apply the employee choice doctrine and will instead determine whether to uphold the employee's forfeiture of benefits based on whether the restrictive covenant was reasonable.

22.7.3. The Non-Competition Provision – The "Unique Employee Doctrine"

Some courts will protect an employer from competition by a former employee whose services are unique or extraordinary. Originally, this rule was applied only to employees with "special talents" such as musicians, professional athletes, actors and writers. At its core, the unique employee doctrine is used to prevent former employees from working for a competitor when the employee has developed "unique" services or has a unique relationship with the employer's customers. Courts applying the rule have expanded the classes of employees against whom those courts will enforce the doctrine from the limited "special talents" categories.

22.7.4. The Non-Competition Provision – The "Inevitable Disclosure Doctrine"

Even in the absence of a specific contractual obligation that restricts your right to work for a competitor, you might find yourself at the end of a lawsuit which has – and is intended to have – the same effect as a non-compete.

Go back to the example above involving the bio-tech scientist. However, now assume that the scientist has no contractual restriction (either in his employment contract or separation agreement) that limits his right to work for a competitive bio-tech company. While that should be the end of the inquiry, it may not be. Companies are increasingly turning to the courts seeking either to enjoin former employees from assuming a position at a competitor or to restrict the duties of the former employee at his new job by invoking the doctrine of "inevitable disclosure."

The entire concept of a non-existent contractual non-compete gets turns on its head in those states where the courts have adopted the "Inevitable Disclosure Doctrine". The fundamental assumption underlying this rule is that the scientist in our example (or other employee on the receiving end of this claim) has a great deal of knowledge about certain trade secrets and confidential information of his former employer.

By applying the inevitable disclosure doctrine, courts can prevent the misappropriation of trade secrets and confidential information based on the assumption that an employee in the specific situation at issue will inevitably use or disclose those secrets (*i.e.* doing so will inherently be required in order for the employee to perform his new job). The rule may be applied even where there is no evidence that the employee intends to use or has used those trade secrets in his new job – intent is not the standard. The rule assumes that if the employee will be unable to function in his capacity for the new employer without disclosing or using his former employer's trade secrets or confidential information, the former employer may obtain an injunction prohibiting the former employee from working in his new position.

Courts that will entertain an application for an injunction by a former employer may consider a variety of factors including, by way of example, one or more of the following:

- ▶ Whether the new employer is a competitor of the old

- ▶ Scope of the employee's new job versus his old job

- ▶ Whether the former employer can identify specific trade secrets that are at risk of disclosure

- ▶ Whether the employee signed a non-disclosure and/or non-competition agreement

- Steps the former employer has taken to protect its trade secrets

- Whether the employee's new position can be circumscribed to eliminate the risk of disclosure

The doctrine is predicated upon the assumption that once a trade secret or confidential information is disclosed, the genie cannot be put back into the bottle. Thus, courts generally will not grant injunctive relief to a former employer under the inevitable disclosure doctrine where the disclosure has already occurred or where future harm is merely speculative.

Likewise, the rule typically is not used where a trade secret is taken in tangible form (*e.g.* a computer run; document, flash drive, etc.) as contrasted with "in head" intellectual knowledge, since an injunction under a different theory may be appropriate with respect to the tangible items. As in all cases where an injunction is sought, the former employer will also be denied an injunction where the employer can be compensated monetarily for the injury or loss it alleges it will suffer.

22.7.5. *Consequences Of Former Employer's Attempt To Seek Injunctive Relief*

There are a variety of reasons why employers send their lawyers into court to seek an injunction prohibiting a departing employee from soliciting other employees or firm customers, or disclosing trade secrets or confidential information, or going to work for a competitor. Sometimes, the employer has demonstrable proof that a former employee is engaged in conduct specifically prohibited in an agreement with the employee and the former employer can establish that the conduct will cause significant harm to the employer which can't be fixed later.

Sometimes, the employer has a genuinely held good faith belief (but no hard proof) that the former employee is, or is about to engage in such proscribed conduct. Or the former employer has a "gut" feeling that something is happening and is sure that the former employee must be the antagonist and wants it stopped!

Sometimes the employer – without any solid factual basis – improperly uses litigation as tool to tie up its former employee in legal proceedings and make him spend money on a lawyer and litigation expenses in order to impede the employee's job search. Or perhaps to slow down the employee from getting a fast start at his new employer. In reality, the motivation behind the former employer's efforts to try to obtain an injunction may be to interfere with the employee's new employment by driving a wedge between the employee and the new employer

Regardless of the former employer's motivation, there may be a serious problem for an employee if his new employer gets involuntarily enmeshed (either as a party or witness) in the litigation. It almost does not matter whether it happens by design (*i.e.* your former employer initiates litigation hoping that your new employer will distance itself from you, thereby keeping you out of the market or buying sufficient time for your former employer to regroup before you actively compete). Or because it is the natural consequence of commencing legal proceedings against a former employee. Either way, there is a serious risk that involving a new employer in litigation between you and your former employer is not going to have a happy ending.

It is possible that your new employer will stand behind you, particularly if you were smart enough to negotiate that type of protection into your new employment agreement. Alternatively, it may decide to terminate your employment or place you on a leave of absence until you can return unencumbered. Maybe it will be a paid leave of absence; maybe not.

At more senior levels, prospective employers will likely ask you for an affirmative representation that its hiring of you will not run afoul of any promise or agreement that you have with any prior employer. You will also be asked to represent that you are not under any type of contractual or judicial restraint that might affect, impair or limit your ability to accept the new position and perform the duties of the job for which you are being hired. Since a new employer probably does not want to start its relationship with you by becoming enmeshed in litigation, there may be a serious impediment to the job offer if you are unable to answer those questions affirmatively.

As a result, all proposed limitations on your post-employment activities must be very carefully reviewed to balance legitimate, protectable interests of your former employer while, at the same time, not unduly hampering your ability to move on.

Litigation often produces an unsatisfactory result even when you are successful in defending yourself.

Unfortunately, this is one area where you can win the battle but lose the war in the process.

22.8. Confidentiality

The fourth type of post-separation restriction involves your promise of confidentiality. There are two categories of confidentiality: the first deals with the separation agreement itself and its terms (discussed below); the second relates to an employer's expectation of confidentiality that is memorialized in the agreement along with the obligation to maintain confidentiality that is recognized under common law, even in the absence of an agreement.

When drafting an employment contract or separation agreement, your employer can denominate anything it wants as "confidential": its ideas, documents, thoughts, papers and all kinds of "other stuff". A confidentiality provision in the separation agreement may carry forward or incorporate the same or similar type of provision that was contained in your original employment contract or published elsewhere by your employer.

Alternatively, the confidentiality provision in the separation agreement may seek to create a new obligation when there is no pre-existing restriction that protects your employer from your post-separation disclosure activities. Such a new restriction may be co-extensive with or exceed your common law obligations or it may seek to build upon an existing confidentiality agreement that you already have with your employer.

As noted, it is not uncommon for an employer to claim that virtually every idea; every sheet of paper; and every shred of information that is created or exists within its corporate universe is a highly valuable business asset and to declare that they all constitute 'confidential information'. By asking you to promise to maintain confidentiality on a broad basis, what your employer really is doing is trying to enlarge its everyday common law legal rights by trying to bind you to a contractual obligation.

However, just because your employer claims that something is confidential does not make it so. And it may make a world of difference when your employer is seeking to have a court enforce a confidentiality provision. The law does not necessarily see things exactly as your employer does and will not enforce a confidentiality 'blank check'.

As a result, a promise of confidentiality, including an agreement by you not to disclose or utilize broadly described categories (but probably lacking in specificity) of information should be carefully reviewed in order to make sure that the separation agreement limits the nature and scope of information to which your employer is entitled to protection. This is a good place to apply the *Rule of 15*. A sloppily drafted provision that leaves you scratching your head as to what you can use or disclose fails the *Rule of 15* and may even unreasonably restrict your right to earn a living.

The clearer and narrower the definition of confidential information in the separation agreement, the easier it will be for a lawyer to advise you whether your proposed conduct falls on the right side of the line drawn by the agreement if the issue should arise. That may, or may not, be the same thing as whether your employer can get a court to enforce the separation agreement and prohibit your conduct. And it may be something entirely different from whether your employer will cease making severance payments to you because it believes you have broken your promise of confidentiality. But it is the right place to start.

Since clarity and specificity are the rule, you should be extremely cautious about agreeing to a confidentiality provision that is vague, undefined and susceptible to multiple interpretations – *see Rule of 15*. To the extent that you and your employer have different understandings and expectations concerning your confidentiality obligations under the agreement, one of you is likely to be disappointed.

Thus, unless there is a good reason for doing so, you should resist efforts to have the separation agreement expand the scope of protection that the law already affords your employer. The law should provide sufficient protection for your employer. To the extent that a document, or data, or information is accurately assessed as confidential, and has been treated as such by your employer, the law will likely protect your employer from your use of that information even in the absence of a confidentiality provision in the separation agreement.

Conversely, a confidentiality undertaking should not apply to documents and information that are accessible in the public realm (*e.g.* the internet, newspapers, trade journals, etc.), and those documents that are personal to your employment such as your performance evaluations, job duties, and those relating to your compensation and benefits. At the risk of being overly simplistic, the test is easy: if a third party can access the information from any source other than your employer's internal files, it should not be subject to a contractual promise of confidentiality.

Example:

> Separation agreements often contain such language as: 'You agree not disclose or utilize any information relating to the business, its activities or Employee's employment . . .' While such phrasing may initially appear benign, literal compliance could effectively render you unemployable.
>
> Does the language mean that you cannot discuss the business of your former employer? Or the nature of your duties and responsibilities for that employer? Or your compensation and benefit related information? One can only cringe at the prospect of the following colloquy when you are interviewing for a new position and you are asked to describe your background, experience and most recent duties and responsibilities:
>
> 'I most recently was employed by XYZ Corp. in the position of _____. Unfortunately, I am not at liberty to discuss what XYZ does or manufactures; nor am I at liberty to discuss or describe the nature of my duties and responsibilities nor any aspect of my compensation from XYZ. But I am confident that I will be a tremendous asset to your organization!'

In sum, your employer will try to obtain broad confidentiality language in your separation agreement. Doing so will, at least in part, provide it with a "club" to hold over your head along with the threat that it carries. The strength of the club is particularly strong if you are supposed to receive ongoing salary continuance or severance payments – those payment may cease if your employer declares that you have somehow breached your promise of confidentiality. That should provide even stronger motivation to carefully review this type of provision.

22.9. The Non-Disclosure Provision

The other type of confidentiality provision relates directly to the separation agreement itself. Separation agreements commonly contain a provision that limits your right to disclose either the existence and/or the particulars of the separation agreement including the payments and other consideration provided to you.

Since most separation agreements are intended to resolve actual, threatened or potential disputes, your employer probably believes that it is paying a premium in order to obtain closure (*i.e.* protection against litigation) and peace and quiet from you. Your employer also wants to try to avoid a possible stampede by other separating employees, now and in the future, who may get ideas from your successful negotiations. This concern is less important in cases involving layoffs or a reduction in force of a number of employees where severance packages are more uniform and are not closely guarded state secrets.

As a result, your employer is loathed to advertise to other employees the extent to which it may go to avoid litigation. Given these concerns, it would be prudent to be quite judicious in discussing your intent to negotiate, or the outcome of your negotiation efforts or your strategy with anyone other than your spouse and lawyer. And that is true even before you have agreed to non-disclosure in the separation agreement. Once the cat is out of the bag and the terms of your separation become common knowledge, the value of confidentiality to your employer is reduced. And that may diminish your leverage in negotiations.

A properly drafted non-disclosure provision should not be objectionable. Except in limited circumstances, you should not have a need to disclose, and your employer is entitled to a comfort level that you won't. That said, you should be sure that the non-disclosure provision includes several carve-outs (exclusions):

> ► There should be no restriction on disclosure to members of your immediate family. 'Family' should be a defined term (*i.e.* spouse, partner, children, siblings, parents, etc.). You should expect that where such disclosure is authorized, the agreement may require that you obtain a promise of the same confidentiality from the person to whom you are making the disclosure.

- Disclosure should be permitted to your lawyer, accountant and tax and financial advisors. Disclosure also should be permitted in connection with other financially related matters (*e.g.* mortgage or refinance applications; matrimonial proceedings, etc.).

- Disclosure of relevant post-employment restrictions (*e.g.* no-solicitation and non-competition provisions) in the separation agreement should be permitted to prospective employers so that you can ensure that you will not be placed in a position where you are unwittingly asked to do something that violates your obligations. It will also ensure that a prospective employer understands the restrictions that will follow you in its employ.

- Disclosure should be permitted in response to a subpoena or other type of legal process. Such exclusions commonly carry an obligation on your part to notify your former employer of your receipt of the subpoena or legal process so that it can take whatever action it deems

> appropriate in order to protect its interests.

- ▶ Disclosure should be permitted in order for you to enforce your rights under the agreement including filing a copy of the agreement with a court to which you make an application for enforcement.

You can ask, but your employer probably will not agree to a mutual promise to limit its right to disclose the agreement and its terms. From your employer's perspective, you should be able to fully control who you talk to concerning the agreement, but your employer may find it difficult to promise non-disclosure by its minions of employees as an institutional matter. However, it should not be a problem for your employer to agree that disclosure will be made only to such officers and senior financial and human resource personnel with a demonstrable need to know. You should attempt to obtain such language particularly if you have reason to be concerned about the risk of any such potential disclosure.

Note: consider whether non-disclosure is one of those issues with a lower priority in your negotiations.

22.10. *The "No Derogatory" Statements Provision*

One of the most vexatious provisions in a separation agreement provisions is the prohibition against you making "derogatory", "disparaging", or "critical" statements concerning the company, its officers, directors, shareholders, employees, products, etc. Some such provisions also prohibit statements that might "injure the reputation" of the company or otherwise harm it.

There may be a world of difference between saying something that can be considered by your former employer as derogatory or critical and statements that are defamatory. Defamatory statements are generally false statements concerning a significant fact. Such statements are not protected by law and you open yourself up to being sued if you make such defamatory statements even if the separation agreement is silent concerning this issue.

In contrast, "derogatory", "disparaging" and "critical" are words without clear definition in law. Indeed, critical, derogatory or even disparaging statement that you might make may not be actionable under state law because they are viewed as "opinion" rather than fact. In reality, they are subjective in the mind of the offended – which is why they are considered more opinion than fact. As such, what is disparaging to your former boss, may just be a joke to someone else. Imagine an analyst or corporate executive commenting to the press concerning a new product being rolled out by his new employer and claiming that it is superior to like products already on the market – one of which is produced by his former employer? Is that disparaging of the former employer's product?

Inasmuch as defamation is a centuries old legal concept that requires a high threshold of proof, there is ample legal precedent that defines where the line between actionable and non-actionable conduct is drawn. That is one of the reasons why your employer is asking for your commitment not to say things that are objectionable to it even if not defamatory. Your employer understands that it likely cannot restrict your right to be critical as a matter of law – as a result, it is trying to create a contract right for itself instead.

The number of ways in which you could unwittingly cross the line are daunting. Under most circumstances, these types of breaches may never become known to your former employer nor will they come back to bite you. Nevertheless, you should attempt to secure language that proscribes only "defamatory" statements or statements that constitute the tort of "product disparagement", another legally recognized and definable concept (*i.e.* unlawfully "bad mouthing" your former employer's products or services). Both of these are likely defined under your state's law. That will allow you to better draw the line between permissible and impermissible conduct more clearly but should also effectively protect whatever legitimate interest your former employer may have.

22.11. *The Successors and Assigns Provision*

Some type of "successors and assigns" provision is standard in any separation agreement. It is important for both you and your employer. In essence, it provides that the agreement will benefit your employer's successors and assigns which means that your obligations will be transferable to any entity that follows in the steps of your employer. That can happen because your employer is sold, merged into, or acquired by another entity which becomes the surviving entity and new owner of your separation agreement.

Hopefully, a successor entity will undertake to meet your former employer's obligations to you under the separation agreement. But that is not necessarily so. It depends upon the type and terms of the transaction that resulted in a successor. Sometimes, it does not really matter. Thus, performance by a successor to your employer may not be terribly important if the only remaining obligations to you are such non-financial obligations as providing a neutral reference (particularly if you already have a new job). However, where there are still outstanding financial payments to be made, you should note that the responsibility to make payment does not automatically become the successor's.

As a result, the separation agreement should permit assignment of the separation agreement to another entity only where that entity agrees to assume your employer's obligations to you and can demonstrate the financial ability to do so. The latter is less important (and less likely that your employer will agree) in the context of large corporate transactions. Alternatively, the agreement could provide for acceleration any unpaid severance or benefits due to you in the event the successor does not provide you with a writing that adopts your separation agreement and contains its agreement to perform its terms including payments. Such a provision will reduce any risk of nonpayment by the successor.

Of course, unless the separation agreement specifically provides to the contrary, the successor or assignee that now owns your agreement also will be entitled to enforce the promises that you made to your former employer as if they had been made to the new entity itself. That may create unanticipated complications. Consider what happens if various promises by you concerning your post-separation activities have largely been ignored by your former employer. Perhaps your employer was favorably disposed to you or maybe the conduct posed no real threat or problem.

But what happens if, some time after your separation, but still during the period of the restrictions, your former employer is acquired by an aggressive company that has a longstanding policy of seeking enforcement of all such contractual provisions. Obviously, this could create unwelcome problems for you. There are limited ways to address these concerns and you should discuss the issue with your lawyer.

Finally, the successors and assigns provision should provide that all payments and benefits that are supposed to accrue to you will be delivered or paid to your heirs or your estate in the event of your death prior to receipt of all of the promised benefits

22.12. *Unemployment Insurance*

The issue of unemployment insurance benefits straddles both the financial and non-financial terms of the separation agreement. Unemployment insurance is a statutory benefit available to individuals who lose their employment and earned income stream through no fault of their own. Your resignation may well disqualify you from receiving unemployment benefits. Periods of eligibility for benefits vary from state-to-state and may be extended by legislative action during periods of high unemployment. Regardless of whether you currently contemplate filing for unemployment insurance benefits, the issue should be addressed in the agreement in the same provision that specifies the reason for separation discussed above. (*See* § 2.2.).

This provision should include the sum and substance of the reason that your employer agrees to provide when asked for that information by the relevant unemployment insurance office:

Example:

> "In response to an inquiry from the state Department of Labor, Unemployment Insurance Division, Employer agrees to state that your employment was terminated involuntarily by Employer [without cause] [due to a corporate reorganization] [due to a reduction in workforce]".

Sometimes, an employer only wants to include language to the effect that it will not contest any application you make for unemployment benefits. Your employer's agreement not to contest your application for benefits – without the additional language above – may not be good enough. To the extent that your employer does not respond to a request from the unemployment office at all, or responds by saying that it does not contest your claim for benefits, you still may be at risk of being denied benefits depending upon the reason that *you* provide for the loss of your job. And it ill-behooves you to falsify your application. You want to be sure that you and your former employer say the same thing.

22.13. References

Depending upon the industry in which you work and your level in the corporate hierarchy, job references have varying degrees of importance. The more senior you are, the less useful and important a written letter of reference will be. Under such circumstances, a prospective employer likely will be able to access top management, SEC filings, news reports, and other public records for an assessment of, or information concerning your job related performance. Indeed, a search of relevant news sites on the internet may tell a prospective employer all it thinks it needs to know.

For less senior workers in industries that are fairly closely knit, prospective employers may also have entre´ to your colleagues and superiors and may seek information concerning you through this network. In larger industries, such access may not be as available. In either event, however, written letters of reference are generally too generic in nature to carry you through the recruitment process and do not have much value as the definitive statement of your work performance. In other words, a letter of reference does not provide much cover.

No matter who you are, your life story may already be an open book if you can be found on Facebook, LinkedIn and other social media venues. In such cases, written references may be virtually valueless.

Most employers will provide only such limited information as dates of employment and last position held in response to a request for a reference. However, if a job reference is an important issue for you, it is helpful to limit the universe of individuals who may speak to an inquiring party to those most likely to be favorable. Accordingly, it will be useful for the separation agreement to specify the company individual who will respond to inquiries concerning your job and work performance.

It probably will be difficult to arrive at an agreed-upon script to be followed by your employer in responding to an inquiry. Do not expend a lot of energy trying to do so. Accept that there are some things you cannot protect against. Even an agreed upon script to be followed by your employer – even assuming that is a good idea – can be delivered to carry any number of messages. Ultimately, it is your name, reputation, experience and demonstrated success that will speak more loudly than anything else.

22.14. *Miscellaneous Provisions*

The following are examples of other provisions commonly found in separation agreements. These provisions often are referred to as 'boiler plate'. Despite the fact that these provisions appear routine, some could have significant implications for you and should be carefully reviewed.

22.14.1. *Miscellaneous Provisions: The Zipper Clause*

The "zipper clause", also is known as an "integration" or "merger" clause. This clause provides that the four walls of the separation agreement reflect the entire understanding and agreement between you and your employer. It likely will also provide that the agreement cannot be changed or modified without a written document that is signed by both you and your employer. In essence, this provision is intended to put you on notice that unless everything you expect – or think – or hope – will happen or be provided to you is addressed in the separation agreement, it is not an enforceable expectation and you should not rely upon it as part of the deal.

Examples:

> "This agreement supersedes all prior written and oral agreements, contracts and understanding between Employee and the Company, all of which are hereby merged into this Agreement with no term or condition of any such agreement surviving execution of this Agreement."

• • •

> "This agreement contains the entire understanding between Employee and the Company. No provision of this agreement may be modified, amended, waived or discharged except as agreed to in a writing signed by both Employee and the Company."

This is not to say, however, that your employer won't honor a verbal deal or understanding that you have with your employer even if it is not addressed in the agreement. It may. Rather, the failure to specifically include such promise in the separation agreement means that it creates no binding obligation on the part of your employer to fulfill the promise. It is the difference between your employer voluntarily doing something as contrasted with doing it because it is obligated to do so.

22.14.2. Miscellaneous Provisions: Severability

Another common provision is referred to as a "severability" provision. In essence, this provision deals with the contingency that a reviewing court or other tribunal finds that a provision of the separation agreement is illegal, void, voidable or unenforceable. This provision attempts to answer the question: "What happens next?" Since there is no single right answer to that question, you should pay careful attention to the drafting of this provision.

Obviously, some provisions in the agreement are more important than others and some may be more important to one party than the other. It is therefore unlikely that a provision of limited or marginal importance ever gets tested in court – it's just not important enough for either party to spend the money to litigate over. Conversely, enforcement of contractual post-employment restrictions on your work and other activities that are contained in a separation agreement may be very important to your former employer if it feels that your conduct is placing its business at some risk (*i.e.* you are soliciting customers or employees in violation of a non-solicitation provision). Or where you violate a limitation on your right to work for a competitor of your former employer.

Suppose the restriction on your solicitation of employees and customers of your former employer is narrowly drafted and not subject to successful legal challenge in court. In that case, you are likely to comply with the terms of the agreement rather than assume the downside risk of being sued by your former employer. But also suppose that the non-competition provision in the agreement is overly broad because it prohibits you from working for a competitor of your former employer in any capacity anywhere in the world. Except in unusual circumstances, a court will not enforce such a provision. Enter the severability provision.

The severability provision is included in agreements to give guidance to a reviewing court as to the parties' intentions and their attempt to preserve the benefit of the bargain between them as completely as possible.

Examples:

> "If any provision of this agreement is invalid or unenforceable, the balance of this agreement will remain in effect."

> • • •

> "It is agreed that in the event any particular provision or provisions of this agreement is or are determined to be illegal, unenforceable or void by a court of competent jurisdiction, such determination shall solely effect such provision or provisions and not impair the remaining provisions of this agreement."

In the absence of a severability provision, the applicable state law will instruct a reviewing court as to the legal consequences that should flow from its determination that a provision must be struck. For example, a court may simply sever the offending provision and enforce the remainder of the agreement without that provision. Of course, that may leave your employer with an agreement which no longer carries the benefit of your promises even though your employer has already provided benefits to you in exchange for those promises. Alternatively, a court might void the entire agreement.

The severability provision represents the parties' attempt to avoid these harsh results. Most commonly, such a provision authorizes a court to rewrite an otherwise unenforceable provision in order to make it legally enforceable. This most frequently occurs in the context of restrictive covenants, confidentiality provisions and no-solicitation restrictions. If the restriction at issue is held to be overly broad, and therefore unenforceable as drafted, the severability provision asks the reviewing court to narrow the time frame, geographic scope or other limitations of the restriction in order to make the provision enforceable against you.

Example:

> "It is agreed that in the event a court of competent jurisdiction shall determine that a provision of this agreement is unenforceable, illegal or void because the scope of the provision (geographic or otherwise) is overly broad, the parties request that the

said court nevertheless enforce each such provision to the fullest extent permissible under applicable law."

While courts generally are loathed to write agreements for the parties, the law also abhors a forfeiture that could otherwise be avoided. The severability clause allows a court to engage in the fiction that it is not re-writing the provision at issue, but, rather it simply is enforcing the contractual provision in accordance with the wishes and intent of the parties.

22.14.3. Miscellaneous Provisions: Choice Of Law, Forum & Venue

Choice of law, forum and venue provisions address the "what", "who" and "where" of dispute resolution concerning the separation agreement. "What" – what law applies. "Who" – who decides the case. "Where" – where the case will be heard.

Example:

> "All questions of validity and interpretation of this agreement, as well as all disputes arising hereunder between Employee and the Company, shall be governed by, construed and enforced in accordance with the laws of the State of _____ and Employee and the Company agree that all such proceedings shall be brought in [the federal or state court] [arbitration before the American

Arbitration Association] sitting in the City of _____, State of _____ which shall be the sole venue for adjudication of disputes between Employee and the Company."

A choice of law provision specifies which state law is to be applied to the interpretation and enforcement of the separation agreement. This is important because the law that governs agreements may vary widely from state-to-state depending upon the issue. Usually, the choice of law designated in the agreement by your employer will be the employer's home state or the state where you were employed.

If you have not yet done so, look for this provision and determine the state law at issue. You should consult with a lawyer who is admitted to practice law and can give you advice as to the law of the state that will govern the agreement. Consulting with an attorney with expertise in New Hampshire law to advise you concerning the legal consequences of provisions in the agreement that are governed by the laws of Alaska is not productive – unless perhaps the New Hampshire lawyer is also admitted to practice law in Alaska. And even then.....

Choice of law is different from the forum designated in the agreement for disputes to be adjudicated – who will hear and decide the case. Generally, the designated forum is limited to federal or state trial courts or to some type of arbitration.

An additional consideration relates to the "venue" – the geographic location where any dispute concerning the separation agreement is required to litigated. Such venue provisions specify the jurisdiction where the case is required to be filed and heard. Venue may be important if your employer has offices or facilities in a number of states. If so, your employer will likely have local counsel in each of these states.

As a result, your employer may have the option of designating different venues for adjudication of disputes – only some of which may be convenient to you or bear any relationship to the dispute. Conversely, your employer may want uniformity of interpretation so that it does not risk having the same provision held to be enforceable in one state, but not in another. If that is a concern, your employer may opt for the same choice of law, forum and venue in all agreements regardless of the state in which you were employed.

In sum, there generally is nothing that prevents a court in Missouri from interpreting your separation agreement in Missouri by applying New Jersey law. Likewise, the separation agreement could provide that the law of Florida will apply, but that all disputes will be heard and decided by a court or arbitrator in Los Angeles County in California – even though you worked in Missouri. It may sound cumbersome, but it's called the employer's home court advantage and courts generally will defer to such contract provisions provided there is some reasonable connection between the parties, the issue in dispute, and the designated forum and venue.

22.14.4. Miscellaneous Provisions: Waiver Of Re-Employment Rights

Separation agreements usually contain a provision that confirms that your employment terminated (or will terminate) as of a specified date. The agreement will likely also contain an explicit waiver by you to re-instatement or re-employment to your former or any other position with your former employer. There may also be language to the effect that you give up any claims that you might have if you seek reinstatement or reemployment despite having agreed not to do so.

Example:

> "Employee acknowledges that his last day of active employment with the Company was _____. Employee waives any and all rights to rehire, re-employment and reinstatement to his current, last, or any other former or other position with the Company and all rights which might otherwise accrue to him in the event he should make application therefore notwithstanding this provision."

This clause is intended to protect your employer from having to do battle with you again, after it resolves all issues surrounding your separation now. However remote, your employer may be concerned that you will accept the financial benefits of the separation arrangement and then apply for re-employment. While it might be a stretch that you would want to go back to work for a firm that has terminated you, your employer undoubtedly has no interest in re-hiring you or having to deal with you again. But, if you apply anyway, and your application is rejected, your employer does not want to worry that you will then sue it under some legal theory by claiming that the refusal to re-hire was in retaliation for your assertion of some legal right that led to the separation agreement. Or because you are too old, the wrong sex, ...

This provision should not create a problem for you. It provides a comfort level to which your employer is entitled, and, unless you are scheming to pursue your employer, it should not matter to you. And, in the unlikely event that a job becomes available for which you are qualified, interested, and for which your former employer wants to re-hire you, the provision in the separation agreement can always be waived.

22.14.5. *Miscellaneous Provisions: Transitional Assistance And Advice*

Depending upon the position you held and the nature of your duties, your employer may seek to require you to assist in transitional or other matters. Sometimes, this obligation is structured to create a consultancy that is intended to preserve access by your employer to your knowledge concerning ongoing and/or historical matters.

Alternatively, the separation agreement may contemplate that your former employer can call upon you from time-to-time to answer transitional business questions or to assist or cooperate with it in the event of any type of investigation, governmental inquiry or litigation. There are a number of considerations that should be evaluated with respect to such a provision.

Initially, the subjective nature of the words "cooperation" and "assistance" is a potential concern. To the extent that you agree to provide cooperation in exchange for financial benefits, you run the risk that your employer might claim to be dissatisfied with the level of your "cooperation". If, from your employer's perspective, it is "buying" your assistance with severance pay, it expects full value from you. As a consequence, your employer may decide to withhold further payments to you or attempt to recover payments already made if its expectations do not match yours.

Language is even more critical with respect to your "cooperation" in connection with an investigation or litigation. Words like "cooperate" and "assist", when used in the context of assisting with litigation and in conjunction with the payment to you of money (*e.g.* severance), may leave the impression that you have been paid for a favorable by-product. Distinguish those words from others such as "make yourself available" or "agree to appear to be interviewed" which are more neutral. You do not want to place yourself in a position where it may appear that your testimony, or favorable cooperation, has been purchased by your employer.

The possibility that "cooperating" in connection with an investigation or a litigation may raise one or more of the following concerns which should be carefully considered:

- You may expose yourself to criminal liability.

- You may expose yourself to civil liability to your former employer. However, depending upon whether you obtained a release from your employer, and the scope and language of that release, this may not be a serious problem.

- You may expose yourself to civil liability to a third party (*e.g.* another employee or someone outside of the company). If that is the case, it may also raise issues as to claims by the third party against the employer which may seek to assert derivative claims against you. *See* discussion above relating to defense, indemnification and releases.

Another consideration relates to the amount of time, and the place where you are required to provide such assistance.

- Is there a limit to the number of hours that you are required to expend?

- Can you be required to travel out-of-town?

- How will you know when the period during which you can be called upon has expired?

- Will you be compensated for your time?

- Will you be reimbursed for expenses that you incur?

- What if there is a conflict with your duties for your new employer?

Even clear language cannot eliminate all of these concerns. Well drafted language, however, can go a long way toward eliminating some of the vagaries:

Examples of language that can limit the scope of your assistance:

"Through _____, Employee will provide assistance to Employer up to _____ hours per week/month on a non-cumulative basis."

• • •

"Matters within the scope of your personal knowledge obtained through the performance of your duties..."

• • •

"Matters in which you were personally involved..."

While these still leave a hole through which "cooperation" can be driven, they are clearly less open-ended than "matters concerning the company's business, activities, customers and employees..."

Finally, there is the possibility that the cooperation requested by your employer may create a conflict with the duties and obligations you owe to your new employer. For example, suppose your former and current employer are competitors or have adverse interests in an ongoing litigation. If your former employer asks for your cooperation, and maybe even your testimony on its behalf in that litigation, you may find that this creates a serious problem for your new employer. It is one thing to be compelled to give testimony if you are served with some type of legal process such as a subpoena; it is quite another to do so voluntarily and to the detriment of your current employer.

One approach is a provision that creates an exception to the cooperation obligation:

> "Consistent with your Employee's and obligations to any employer or business entity with which Employee is then employed, associated, affiliated or involved, Employee shall make himself available to Employer, at reasonable times and places, and subject to non-interference with Employee's then employment or business activities and obligations, to provide information to it concerning Employee's direct knowledge of any aspect of any litigation, arbitration, investigation, governmental proceeding or other proceeding involving Employer in respect of work performed or services rendered by Employee while Employee was employed by

Employer. In connection therewith, Employer agrees to compensate Employee at the per diem rate of $ .00 for each day for which Employee is asked to devote any time and likewise to reimburse Employee for all reasonable out-of-pocket expenses incurred by Employee, including travel expenses."

Or any combination of the foregoing. Alternatively, although probably less acceptable to your employer, consider a provision that requires that a subpoena be issued by your employer compelling your testimony.

23.

Financial Terms Of Separation

Now onto the cash and benefits.

23.1. Earned Compensation

You are entitled to receive compensation if you have satisfied all of the conditions that are a prerequisite to payment and have an unconditional right to be paid. Such earned compensation generally is not subject to forfeiture; once you have earned it, you have a right to payment. That also means that payment of earned compensation is not adequate consideration for any of the promises you make in the separation agreement.

The clearest example of earned compensation are your wages or your salary. When your last day of work, or the next scheduled payday, will occur after your execution of the separation agreement, the agreement should explicitly provide for payment of all salary and related compensation accrued through the last day of work so that there is no question that you have not released payment of that earned compensation. Indeed, in most jurisdictions, such a waiver would likely be void, but getting paid for earned compensation is not something you should have to fight over. And it may not be worth fighting over.

For purposes of clarity, the agreement should specify the exact amount to be paid as well as the date (or outside date) by which such sum will be paid. Of course, payment will be subject to regular payroll tax deductions and charges including deductions for insurance and related payments. The preferred description should be in actual dollars as contrasted with such descriptions as "paid your regular salary". *See Rule of 15.*

In the event that your last day of employment is scheduled to occur after the last date of work, the salary and related compensation attributable to that period likewise should be specified in specific dollar amounts as well as specific dates on which such amounts will be paid:

Example:

"You will paid the sum of $_____ as salary continuation which will be paid to you by the company in _____ equal weekly/bi-weekly installments commencing _____ and ending _____, each such installment in the gross amount of $_____."

Most separation agreements contain a provision in which you acknowledge that you have received and been paid all monies due to you from your employer for or on account of wages, overtime, wage supplements, commissions, bonuses, incentive and deferred compensation, profit sharing, benefits, accrued vacation and expense reimbursement.

Example:

"Employee acknowledges and represents to the Company that, except as otherwise provided in this Agreement, as of the date of his execution of this Agreement, he has been paid all monies due to him from the Company for or on account of wages, overtime, wage supplements, commissions, bonuses, incentive and deferred compensation, profit sharing, benefits, accrued vacation, PTO (paid time off) and expense reimbursement."

Make sure that this statement is true. If there are any unpaid amounts due to you as of the date you execute the separation agreement, be sure that the agreement specifically provides for payment of these outstanding monies. Otherwise, you may forfeit or waive the right to such monies or, at a minimum, have to chase your employer for payment. That includes not only salary, but expense reimbursement, tuition allowances, relocation payments and the like.

23.2. Bonus or Incentive Compensation

Earned compensation is different from bonus or incentive compensation, either of which may be payable solely at the discretion of your employer. Payment maybe in cash or in some combination of cash and/or equity (generally stock and/or options). In addition, incentive compensation may be subject to deferral, either on a voluntary basis on your part for a variety of reasons including tax considerations, or mandatorily by your employer as a way to induce your long term loyalty and employment with the firm (the proverbial "golden handcuffs"). Your employer is entitled to establish the eligibility requirements, amount, vesting, forfeiture events and terms of payment in its sole discretion.

The distinction is important because incentive compensation, as contrasted with earned compensation, generally is viewed under the law as a gratuity payable by your employer pursuant to whatever rules it adopts. But there are even distinctions within the category of incentive compensation. If there is an incentive compensation or bonus plan that provides for specific payments upon the attainment of defined benchmarks (based upon either or both company and/or individual performance), the incentive nature of the bonus may be transformed into earned compensation upon attainment of the requisite benchmark. In contrast, the bonus will retain its status as a gratuity if the bonus plan provides that any bonus that may be awarded will be at the sole discretion of the employer.

Initially, your lawyer should determine whether any of the compensation at issue is earned or incentive. That will define whether you are chasing a right or a gratuity. As part of that analysis, the compensation should be examined to determine whether there is any basis for a claim that you are entitled to a pro-rata share of incentive compensation for the portion of the year during which you are employed. To the extent that the compensation at issue is "incentive" and not earned, there generally is no legal right to be paid a pro rata bonus. Rather, any such argument falls within the scope of *"Aw C'mon"* negotiations. Thus, even if you have worked for 11/12 of the bonus year, you have no legal right to a bonus for that year unless the employer's rules provide for payment of a bonus on a pro rata basis.

One wrinkle. In the financial services industry, employees generally are required to submit any compensation disputes or claims they have with their employer to arbitration. Some non-financial industry employers also require their employees to do so. This may be important because there may be a somewhat different standard that is applied by arbitrators than by judges when adjudicating claims about unpaid incentive compensation or bonus.

In a court of law, you generally should expect that your case will be dismissed if the compensation at issue falls clearly within the "gratuity" category. Courts apply the law to the facts of the case without regard to the inequity or unfairness that the result may cause. Working for 11/12 of the year is irrelevant in court if the incentive plan is a gratuity – the employer is free to do whatever it wants.

The outcome might – but only might – be somewhat different in arbitration where fairness and equity may not be wholly irrelevant to the arbitrator hearing your case. That's because arbitrators are not necessarily bound to follow the strict dictates of the law and may infuse the proceedings with some degree of "humanity". That makes it possible that you could be awarded a pro rata bonus even though you do not have a specific legal right to it.

23.3. Severance And Salary Continuation

Severance is commonly understood to be a payment to you in a specific amount, or for a defined period of time, following the last day of your employment. In contrast, salary continuation connotes keeping you on the employer's payroll with or without duties or responsibilities, until the specified termination date. You could also start on salary continuation and revert to severance sometime thereafter, but generally not in the reverse order. Obviously, severance and salary continuation are the areas where the greatest amount of negotiation generally takes place.

In most jurisdictions, severance and salary continuation are not a right. Any entitlement that you have exists only to the extent it has become a term and condition of your employment by agreement between you and your employer or by virtue of an enforceable policy that has been promulgated by your employer. This is a classic example of a 'deal' exception to the employment at-will rule discussed above. Thus, even in the absence of a statutory obligation to provide severance pay, the law generally will enforce an employer's promise to do so.

Where severance or salary continuation is negotiated on an individual basis with your employer either at the commencement of your employment, or as part of negotiations over renewal of your employment contract, or for any other reason during the term of your employment (*i.e.* a promise of severance in order to induce you to continue in your job pending the closing of a merger or acquisition), the terms of that arrangement will govern.

In addition to traditional employment contracts, severance or severance related rights may be found in 'stay or retention agreements', 'change of control' agreements and other agreements that provide for payments to you upon the occurrence of defined events. These can be individually tailored to your unique situation or more broadly to address specific events. For example, if your employer is trying to sell its business, it may want to induce key employees to stick around until the business is sold by offering all, or a class of employees, a 'stay or retention' bonus to stay with the firm until closing or other specified date.

Severance plans that are not negotiated on an individual basis can range from a formal, written plan that is subject to regulation by the federal Employee Retirement Income Security Act ("ERISA") to an *ad hoc* approach by which your employer makes severance pay decisions on a case-by-case basis, without any one decision being a precedent in any other situation. Provided that decisions as to whether to pay severance are made on a non-discriminatory basis, your employer generally is free to do whatever it wants.

As a result, unilaterally adopted severance plans can impose virtually any condition your employer wishes to impose concerning eligibility and payment of benefits. The following are several examples of some of the more common formulations providing for severance pay:

- ▶ An unconditional promise to pay a specified number of weeks/months of severance per year of employment

- ▶ An unconditional promise to pay a specified number of weeks/months of severance per year of employment up to a maximum amount

- ▶ A promise to pay a specified number of weeks/months of severance per year of employment subject to certain specified conditions (*i.e.* until you find a new job)

- A promise to pay provided that you do not 'compete' for a specified period of time

- A promise to pay provided that you do not solicit/hire your former employer's employees for a specified period of time

- A promise to pay provided that you sign a general release of your rights and claims

- A promise to pay provided that you opt out of a class action

- A promise to pay provided that you agree to provide on-going consultation and advice to the employer

- A promise to pay provided that you agree to be available for transitional services

- A promise to pay severance to be computed to include base salary only, and excluding bonus and incentive compensation

If your employer has an unconditional policy that provides for the payment of severance in fixed amounts, you are entitled to the severance amount without regard to whether you sign a release or separation agreement. It is unconditional because the severance policy does not require that you sign a release or separation agreement or do anything else as a condition to payment of the severance. In lawyer's lingo, your employment provided the consideration for the severance and you have fully performed. Your employer did not have to draft the policy that way, but since it did, the law will enforce it as written.

In order for your employer to attain its underlying goal of bringing closure to its relationship with you by getting you to execute a broad-based general release, it must offer you something of value to which you are not already entitled. In other words, there must be independent consideration provided to you in exchange for your release in the separation agreement or your promise not to sue.

For that reason, it is important for you to determine whether you have an unconditional right, a conditional right, or no right at all to severance. Only by doing so can you properly evaluate whether your employer's offer to pay you severance is supported by adequate consideration – are you getting something of value in exchange for what you are giving your employer?

Examples:

- ► Your employer has promulgated a severance policy that provides for unconditional payment of 1 week of severance for each completed year of service. You are laid off after 5 years of service and are entitled to 5 weeks of severance under the policy. Your employer cannot condition payment of the 5 weeks of severance on your signing a release. If the promise to pay is unconditional, then your employer cannot add a condition to payment after the fact.

► Same facts, except your employer offers 10 weeks of severance if you sign a release. Under those circumstances, you are entitled to 5 weeks of severance under the policy regardless of whether you sign a release. The promise to pay the additional 5 weeks of severance is the consideration for your release.

► Same policy, except instead of being unconditional, the policy specifies that you are entitled to the 5 weeks of severance only if you sign a release and agreement not to sue. In that case, the offer to pay you 5 weeks of severance is the stated consideration for the release. Without the release, you are not entitled to severance.

Thus, where severance is an unconditional 'right' under a corporate policy, it is not uncommon for an employer to add additional severance to which you are

not otherwise entitled as the 'carrot' for your execution of the release. In reality, the additional severance is less a generous gesture by your employer and, instead, is intended to satisfy the legal requirement that independent consideration be provided to you in order to make your release valid.

Where your employer offers adequate consideration in exchange for your release, care must be taken to properly define the circumstances under which such additional severance will be paid. Among the more common conditions (in addition to those referenced above) that employers attach to payment of severance include a requirement that you search for new employment and periodically report your efforts back to your employer. If that is a condition, then the separation agreement should specify whether the unpaid severance will cease, continue, or be accelerated with the remaining amounts paid to you in a lump sum when you secure new employment.

Where you have a choice, consider whether to structure the severance as a single, lump sum payment or to receive payment on an ongoing regular payroll basis. There are both practical as well as tax considerations. As a general rule, a lump sum payment will result in the immediate termination of your status as an employee. That may also mean that employer paid health insurance and other employee benefits likewise will cease. That might not be the case if you are carried in some employee status during a period of salary continuation. Moreover, and since severance payments may straddle more than one tax year, you should consult your accountant or tax advisor as to the structure that will address your situation and be the most tax efficient for your purposes.

This consideration also raises one of the earlier issues discussed concerning attorneys' fees. If your fee agreement with your lawyer provides for payment of his contingent fee upon settlement, you might find that you owe the lawyer an amount that you may not have or which might wipe out the first several severance payments. Alternatively, you will probably feel the bite out of severance payments made over time less if your lawyer gets paid out of each separate severance payment.

There is an important, but often overlooked practical consideration as well. Receipt of a lump sum payment may allow you to bring psychological closure to the trauma of termination more rapidly than if you are waiting at the mailbox each week to see whether your employer has lived up to its agreement and sent you the next severance pay installment. That problem may be aggravated as the period of severance gets longer.

As with accrued salary, once the specific severance amount is negotiated, the agreement should particularize the specific sum to be paid along with specified dates for payments. *See Rule of 15*. Phrases like "the company will pay your regular salary" should be avoided in favor of specific dollar amounts:

Example:

"During the period commencing and ending on, you will receive the total sum of $_____ payable in equal (weekly/

bi-weekly/monthly) installments, each in the amount of $."

The separation agreement should specify whether the severance payments are eligible for purposes of 401k contributions and whether your employer will continue to match plan contributions made by you during the payment period. Similarly, with respect to your participation in other benefit plans.

23.4. Deferred Compensation

The term deferred compensation plan has a generic meaning to executives and other plan participants, and quite another, technical meaning, to lawyers, accountants and benefit consultants. For purposes of this discussion, the term includes all types of benefit plans in which monies or company equity reside, but which do not necessarily belong to you until some date or event in the future. These may be deferrals from your own earnings, or contributions made to a plan on your behalf by your employer, or a combination of both.

As a general rule, if the monies represent *already earned* compensation, the law generally will protect you from suffering a forfeiture of any part of these monies as a result of your separation – regardless of the reason. However, that assumes that the monies at issue are, in fact, already earned by you. While that distinction may seem straightforward, there are sophisticated legal nuances that may change the applicable legal landscape dramatically. As a result, you may find that you are negotiating (or litigating) over monies that you had always believed were yours, but about which there now is some dispute.

Where there is an enforceable agreement with your former employer regarding compensation, the status of these monies should be easily discernible if the agreement is clear as to what you earn; how you earn it; and when and under what circumstances it is paid to you. Unfortunately, many of these writings or agreements lack sufficient clarity and become the subject of dispute and litigation over the core issue of whether the compensation is earned. *See Rule of 15.*

Most commonly, disputes over deferred compensation involve questions concerning whether an employee participant has a vested, non-forfeitable right to some or all of the deferred compensation. Inasmuch as the deferred compensation plan likely was the product of your employer's unilateral drafting and implementation (rather than an arm's length negotiation with you), the terms of the plan may provide for forfeiture upon the occurrence of any one or more contingent events. Even certain vested rights may result in forfeiture (*i.e.* forfeiture of vested, but unexercised stock options upon termination of employment).

By way of example, the deferred compensation plan or arrangement may provide for forfeiture in the event of a voluntary resignation; a voluntary termination without required advanced notice; voluntary termination but subsequent employment during a defined period with a competitor; involuntary termination without cause; involuntary termination for cause; involuntary termination due to death or disability; or termination in the event of a change in control. Depending upon whether there is a significant amount at risk, this may be a ripe area for negotiation if, by redefining the termination event, you are able to resurrect deferred compensation rights that might otherwise be subject to forfeiture.

Your attorney should review each deferred compensation plan in which you are a participant to determine your rights under each such plan. There likely are booklets, or plan or award documents that detail your status and rights. While the general rule is that you should be fully vested in your own contributions to these plans, there is some case law that suggests that a plan can lawfully be drafted by an employer to provide for a forfeiture of even your own contributions into such plan.

Moreover, if your deferred compensation has been invested in some vehicle such as the company's stock or a basket of mutual funds, the plan may require that you cash out and withdraw your vested, non-forfeitable holdings upon termination or within some narrowly defined time period following termination. As a result, there is risk that the value of your holdings will be at a diminished level at an inopportune time.

You should also determine the vesting and forfeiture rules applicable to employer-matching contributions to plans in which you are a participant. In the event you are not vested in these contributions, you should determine the amount of time required in order for such vesting to occur. It may be possible to close a relatively short gap in time before vesting occurs by negotiating an adjustment of your last day of employment or by corporate action by a compensation committee of the Board of Directors. Some employers are willing to accelerate vesting under certain of these plans in order to provide additional benefits to departing employees.

Be sure to involve your accountant or tax advisor in analyzing the best way to handle the deferred compensation issue in order to ensure that payments to you with respect to such plans are accorded proper tax treatment and you do not suffer an unexpected, or disadvantageous tax consequence flowing from distributions or payments from such plans. Most employers are willing to accommodate your tax situation consistent with their business and legal obligations.

As with equity grants discussed elsewhere, you should ask your employer to attach a schedule to the separation agreement (which generally can be accomplished with a simple computer generated run) of your holdings, vested and unvested, under each deferred compensation plan in which you are a participant to reduce the potential for dispute later as to your entitlements.

23.5. Vacation

Vacation is not generally a benefit that an employer is required to provide by law – another example of a "gratuity". As a result, vacation is either a matter of agreement between you and your employer or a benefit unilaterally granted by your employer. To the extent that vacation is not a term incorporated in an employment contract, the right to vacation, if any, likely is derivative of a corporate policy addressing this subject. In either event, it is the contract of employment or corporate policy that will specify the manner in which vacation is earned and accrued. Where the vacation policy is not integrated in an employment contract, some states require that employers provide employees with written specification of its vacation, sick and personal leave and holiday policies.

You should review applicable vacation provisions to determine the amount of vacation time that you have accrued and is due to be paid to you (after taking into account any vacation time actually taken) at time of separation. When the last day of employment is not coextensive with the last day of work, it is possible that additional vacation time may accrue simply by passage of time during the period of salary continuation. This issue should be considered in determining your entitlements. Likewise, you should determine whether you are entitled to payment for accrued, unused vacation days even if you do not sign a separation agreement or release.

Once your vacation entitlement has been determined, it should be reduced to a fixed sum in the separation agreement along with a specified outside date by which payment will be made, ordinarily upon signing the agreement or in the next payroll period. Try to avoid phrases like "you will be paid all unused vacation as soon as practicable. . ." – it fails to satisfy the *Rule of 15*.

23.6. Sick/Personal Leave

As with vacation time, sick and personal leave time generally are not required by law, but may be subject to the requirements of the federal Family and Medical Leave Act and similar state law provisions. Your entitlement, if any, to sick or personal leave time, paid or not, is defined by the understandings between you and your employer or the rules unilaterally promulgated by your employer.

The discussion above with respect to calculation of vacation entitlements and accruals applies equally with respect to sick and personal leave and should be similarly analyzed to determine whether any such rights attach at termination of employment and, if so, how to value these rights. To the extent that you are entitled to be paid for any earned, accrued and unused sick or personal leave, the amount and timing of payment likewise should specifically be included in the separation agreement.

23.7. Pension And Retirement Plans

As with the deferred compensation plans, your lawyer should review all of the retirement and pension plans in which you are a participant in order to determine your rights under each of these plans. Special emphasis should be given to determine whether there is a shortfall in service that might dramatically impact your retirement benefits. Where such a shortfall or gap exists, as with deferred compensation plans, your employer may be receptive to crediting you with additional years of service in order to bridge the gap and provide you with greater retirement benefits. Most employers (or the plan administrators) will cooperate with your requests for computer profiles of various possible benefit entitlements based upon various age and years of service combinations.

The particulars of these possible age/service combinations also should be reviewed with your accountant and tax advisors. A computer run or other form should be annexed to the separation agreement detailing your benefits rights under the final arrangement with your employer, based upon the agreed upon age, years of service, and related plan data. All of these terms should be incorporated into the separation agreement with specificity. The value of such an attachment to the separation agreement is that it brings a complicated area closer to the umbrella of the *Rule of 15*. Such inclusion should reduce confusion and misunderstanding as to the level of benefits that you will receive under these plans as well as the date on which you expect to start receiving those benefits.

Given the significant sums involved, it is prudent to take the extra step and be sure that both you and your employer have the same understandings and expectations.

23.8. Health And Medical Insurance

The potential for loss of health and related medical and hospitalization insurance coverage as the result of your separation can have a profound impact on you and your family. The monthly insurance premium costs attributable to procuring comparable coverage on an individual basis in the open marketplace may prove to be quite expensive and potentially prohibitive. Indeed, some insurance coverage may even be unavailable, or accord you far less coverage than you require or enjoyed during your employment.

There are three basic sources in evaluating post-separation insurance rights. First, your lawyer should review any contract of employment between you and your employer in order to determine what, if any, contractual rights you might have to health and related insurance following separation. Such benefits may be defined in a class based manner: "You will be provided with such health, medical . . . benefits as are provided, from time-to-time, by the Company to managing directors/vice-presidents/senior executives, etc."

Alternatively, the benefit entitlement may be specifically identified by contract, which generally occurs in the case of senior executives and those employees for whom such insurances provide a mechanism for significantly supplementing their cash compensation.

The second source that should be reviewed is your employer's internal policies. In the case of an at-will employee – regardless of level – such policies are likely to be the only source in which to find a benefit entitlement. These policies may be found in an employee handbook, personnel manual, management rulebook, or benefit booklets (sometimes referred to as Summary Plan Descriptions).

Many such policies provide for benefit continuation following separation based upon specified considerations. These benefits may be provided at the employer's costs, your cost, or on a cost-sharing basis. As discussed above, you should determine the date on which your current insurance coverage ceases inasmuch as the date of cessation could be the last day of work; last day of employment; or even the last day of the month in which the termination occurs.

The third source of information is applicable statutes such as the federal Consolidated Omnibus Budget Reconciliation Act commonly referred to as 'COBRA' and mini-COBRA statutes on the state level that provide for benefit continuation by separating employees. COBRA is intended to accord separating employees (and other defined classes of persons) with the right to continue coverage under their employer's group policy even after employment terminates.

COBRA coverage is not a free ride, but it should provide a significant savings. Your employer is entitled to charge you the same premium rate that it incurs for its active employees, plus a nominal additional charge for administrative expenses. Thus, if you opt for COBRA coverage, you get the same health insurance coverage that is available to active company employees, but at the premium rate your employer was able to negotiate for itself on a group-wide basis. This generally will be available to you for 18 months following termination of your employment, or until such time as you become covered under another health insurance policy, whichever occurs first. You should check to see if either the U.S. Congress or the state legislature relevant to you has provided for extended continuation benefits or subsidized cost.

There are certain exceptions to your right to COBRA benefits. These include a termination of employment for gross misconduct. In such cases, you may be denied to the right to COBRA coverage. As a result and where continued health insurance coverage is a high priority for you, this is yet another reason why the nature of your separation, and the way it is denominated in the separation agreement, should be carefully negotiated. In addition, certain statutory provisions could limit the extent of your coverage such as where the group coverage provided by your employer itself changes.

Note that there are significant changes to heath care benefits that are scheduled to kick in starting in 2014. Depending upon the final form of these changes, you may have to adjust your negotiating strategy accordingly.

Health insurance can be an expensive benefit especially if you have received family coverage at your employer's sole cost. While your visceral instinct may be to try to negotiate for your employer to pay your monthly insurance premiums for an extended period, this is not necessarily the best financial play. In addition to these considerations discussed above, also consider the following:

- Whether you intend to re-enter the workforce
- Whether you are entitled to retiree health insurance benefits (if retirement is an option that you are seriously considering)
- Whether you are Medicare eligible
- The cost of paying the premiums yourself
- Your expected period of unemployment

As was also discussed above, each component of a financial separation package consumes a slice of an overall pie that your employer is prepared to spend on your separation. Health insurance can become a disproportionately expensive slice of the pie.

For example, if you successfully negotiate employer paid health insurance continuation for one year after termination and you find a new job with comparable health insurance benefits in 3 months, you have negotiated – and bought – a 12 month benefit with only a 3 month value because you become covered under your new employer's plan. This may render most of the benefit continuation you negotiated moot.

Thus, you may find that even a modest amount of additional severance will more than compensate for the actual cost to you of COBRA coverage and may even provide a windfall in the event you find employment sooner than you expect. You should compute the number of months of insurance premiums that one month of severance can buy taking into account the appropriate tax considerations. That may give you an idea of where your negotiating emphasis should lie.

A word of caution is in order. If health insurance is of paramount importance for any reason, you should concentrate your negotiations on the date of commencement of COBRA coverage. Where the separation agreement provides that your last day of work is also the date of termination, COBRA eligibility will probably commence as of that date or the beginning of the month following termination. Once the 18 month COBRA continuation period begins, it does not matter whether you, or your employer, pays the monthly insurance premium. Regardless of who pays the premium, each month is charged against your 18 month COBRA entitlement.

However, where the termination date is the last day of the period of salary continuation (during which you are continued in some employee classification so that you can continue to qualify for benefits as if nothing had changed), the 18 month COBRA eligibility period may start then. Since you generally are entitled to 18 months of COBRA coverage, you want the 18 month clock to start ticking as late as possible so that you are covered for the longest period.

For example, if you are able to negotiate for continued coverage during a 6 month period that you are on salary continuation, then you should try to specify that the 18 month COBRA period will not begin until the 6 months of "pre-termination" coverage ends. In that case, you have the potential for 24 months of coverage for which your employer pays the first 6 months and you pay the last 18 months of premiums.

23.9. Outplacement

Outplacement firms provide an opportunity and benefit for both you and your employer. This benefit is almost always provided at your employer's cost – which means that the benefit is consuming a slice of the severance/separation pie. The cost of outplacement services can range from relatively modest to quite expensive.

The actual cost incurred by your employer will be driven by a number of factors, including whether the outplacement firm has some type of retainer or fixed fee arrangement with your employer, or is engaged on an assignment basis. Larger employers and those experiencing significant downsizings are more likely to have the retainer type relationship. If so, there may be no, or only a marginal cost to your employer to provide outplacement services for you.

It is not unusual for an employer to immediately introduce a separating employee to an outplacement counselor following notification of the termination of employment. In part, the counselor is there to provide assistance in your transition; in part, the counselor's role is to cushion the impact of the news that your employer just delivered.

From your employer's perspective, it hopes that the outplacement process provides focus in your job search efforts and structure to your day. However, it is not pure benevolence. Rather, your employer is hopeful that you are successful in securing a new position sooner, rather than later, and in focusing your time and energies on tomorrow rather than on yesterday – even if you have signed a release.

Some separating employees find outplacement very valuable; it gets them out of the house and allows them to continue their routine of going to an office and working for several hours during each day. Others feel that quality outplacement service provides invaluable assistance with their job search. Yet other employees find that networking and headhunters are the best way to spend their time looking for a new position. There is no right answer; you should evaluate your personal needs and circumstances.

If you decide that outplacement is not of value to you, you might try asking your employer to give you the cash value or cost of the outplacement in lieu of providing the benefit to you. Since there are tax considerations, don't be blinded by the cash. When in doubt, use outplacement unless you are confident of its limited value.

Assuming that you will find outplacement services to be valuable, the separation agreement should specify the name of the outplacement firm and the office location(s) at which the services will be provided. You might want to research various outplacement firms or seek a recommendation from a colleague who had a favorable experience and propose that firm to your employer. If your employer proposes outplacement services at a specific location that is not convenient for you, you should reserve the right to use any of the outplacement firm's offices.

An important issue is the level of services being offered. Most outplacement firms offer different levels of service to their business clients seeking to refer separating employees. The separation agreement should identify the specific level of service to be provided (*e.g.*basic, executive, senior executive, etc.). If the time period during which the services will be provided is not inherent in the specified level (outlined in the firm's brochure provided to you), the applicable time period also should be spelled out. The more basic the level of service, the shorter the time during which it will be available. And, if outplacement will be available for only a limited period, you should consider whether you want to start the clock running immediately, or at some later date so that holiday periods and generally slow hiring seasons do not eat up the outplacement period. The separation agreement should specify the details.

The outplacement firm undoubtedly will assist you in preparing a new resume and work with you to develop a skills assessment analysis to identify where your strengths lie and job search efforts should be directed. Depending on the level of service for which your employer has contracted, the firm may also make an office available for your use, and provide you with telephone, fax and related office and clerical services, conduct networking clinics and provide you with access to on-line databases.

One final word concerning outplacement. The decision to provide outplacement is motivated, at least in part, by corporate self-interest. The outplacement firm and your assigned counselor are part cheerleader, shrink, headhunter, and shoulder to lean on. The faster, and more positive your transitional experience, the better for your employer.

The corollary is that the outplacement firm is employed by (and paid) your employer – even though it provides services to you. As a result, conversations between you and your outplacement counselor are not protected by any type of privilege. The counselor may have the wisdom of Solomon, but don't be fooled – your conversations with him are not cloaked with confidentiality or with the same type of privilege accorded to conversations with members of the clergy or your lawyer or even your shrink.

As a consequence, you should be judicious about what you discuss with, and disclose to your outplacement counselor. For example, you should consider whether your interests are best served by telling your counselor that you are thinking about taking a few months off to clear your head before you start looking for work – especially if continued severance payments are contingent upon your good faith efforts to secure new employment. The counselor has no need to know most of this information and, under normal circumstances, you should not confide such matters to an outsider.

That said, the savvy negotiator may find that the well placed 'tid-bit' of information with an outplacement counselor may produce dividends. Consider the impact that the well-timed, following off-hand comment by you to your outplacement counselor might have on negotiations with your employer:

Example:

> "I thought that as time went by, I would grow less angry about being fired! But time has not healed my wounds. I'm really pissed. After all of the good, hard years I gave to the Company, the best they could do was offer me a measly 6 months severance. Maybe I should call a well known employment lawyer – I'll bet that he would agree that I've been screwed. The company wouldn't have done this to me if I was [10 years younger] [been a man instead of a woman] . . . etc."

Suppose your comments were then conveyed back to your employer! You might find that the counselor, in a subsequent session, invites you to vent even further and describe your desired package – all in the interests of catharsis, of course. However, this is not the time to shoot from the hip; your discussions should be carefully scripted with your attorney in order to accord you maximum effect.

This may not be the typical mode of negotiating a separation package but when the opportunity presents itself, it can be quite effective. To the extent that you can use the counselor as a conduit (preferably without alerting him that you are doing so) to channel information along with your 'outrage' to your employer, this may provide your employer with an opportunity to step up to the plate without the formality of lawyer initiated discussions.

24.

Getting Ready To Sign The Agreement

As you read through the proposed separation agreement offered by your employer, you may have a sense that it is very forthcoming in trying to do the right thing. Among other things, the agreement may suggest that you consult with a lawyer concerning the agreement; it may tell you that you have 21 or more days to decide whether to sign the agreement; and it may say that you have another 7 days, even after you signed the agreement – to change your mind about entering into the agreement. These provisions are in addition to highlighting the benefits that are being offered to you, along with a reminder that you are not entitled to these benefits unless you sign the agreement.

These provisions are not magnanimous gestures by your employer. During the early 1990's, Congress enacted legislation to curb and deal with abuses by employers in obtaining releases from terminated employees. Often, employers advised employees that their employment was being terminated and immediately presented them with a separation agreement or release to sign in exchange for a severance check. Given the trauma of the situation, employees often signed the release, cashed their severance check and then ran to lawyers who, in turn, filed lawsuits claiming that the releases were not voluntarily signed. Needless to say, the havoc that these lawsuits created in the judicial system sounded a cry for Congressional action.

As a result, federal legislation and regulations now require that certain information be provided in some separation agreements if an employer wants to be able to enforce the release: the proposed agreement needs to be written in understandable language, you are to be advised to consult with a lawyer and you are to be given a minimum of 21 days in which to sign the agreement and another 7 days after you sign the agreement to change your mind. Generally these rule apply only if you are 40 years of age or older, but many employers now regularly include these provisions in all separation agreements.

A fair question to ask your lawyer is whether there is any risk in aggressively trying to negotiate the severance package during the 21 day period that the proposed agreement provides for you to review the document and decide whether to sign it. Certain of these considerations are discussed above and, in part, the answer may depend upon what the proposed agreement says.

Under the law of most states, an offer is just that – an offer. And, in addition to the requirement that the agreement be supported by adequate consideration (discussed above), another basic concept in contract law is that there is no binding agreement until an offer has been accepted – evidence that there is a meeting of the minds between you and your employer. The proposed separation agreement is your employer's offer; your signature is your acceptance. As a result, and unless the offer provides to the contrary, the offer generally can be withdrawn by your employer until you have accepted it by signing the agreement. There may be exceptions to that general rule, but if you intend to rely upon such an exception, make sure your lawyer has signed off on your plan.

Thus, just because you have been given 21 days in which to review the proposed agreement does not necessarily also mean that you have an irrevocable option for that 21 day period. As unlikely as it may be, it is possible that the proposed agreement may be withdrawn by your employer before the 21 days expire.

Afterward

Even the most carefully crafted agreement ultimately relies upon the good faith of the parties to effect compliance with the deal and understanding between them. Litigation and disputes that flow from unclear or omitted provisions in an agreement are unfortunate, but rarely is there an agreement that is so clear that all parties still agree upon the meaning of all of the provisions well after the fact.

More troublesome are disputes over unmet expectations – where there is no dispute as to what the employer had agreed to do; it just failed or refused to do it. Sometimes, the employer claims that it is relieved of its obligations to comply because of your conduct during the intervening period.

Most employers will not take the time and effort, and spend the money to negotiate an agreement that they intend to abrogate. But the hard reality is that it is virtually impossible to walk away from an executed agreement and be sure that your former employer will fully comply with it. Your employer's history and your relationship with it may strongly suggest a low risk road ahead; or maybe not. Remember, after all is said and done, neither you nor lawyer can force your employer to comply with its obligations – even obligations that are crystal clear. Only a judge, arbitrator or someone else vested with the force of law can accomplish that end. The cost of getting there, however, means that you may have lost, even if you are victorious.

There are only a limited numbers of options to deal with this concern. The best, of course, it to negotiate to get all of the cash and benefits paid to you up-front, upon signing the agreement or as soon as it is effective. For what it's worth, that puts you in the position of being the 'chased' (if the employer believes you have violated the agreement) rather than the chaser! Perhaps your employer is less likely to sue you for perceived violations of the agreement than it will be to stop making payments to you.

Second, you can attempt to negotiate a provision that requires your employer to pay the cost of obtaining its compliance with the terms of the agreement including payment of your attorney's fees and related courts costs and expenses. While this may not change the need for a 'chase', it may make it more likely that your employer will think twice about not complying with its obligations because it will have to pay your cost of the chase as well as its own. The larger the employer, the less material that amount becomes. At the same time, the larger the employer, the less likely it is that it will sign an agreement and then simply refuse to comply.

Employers generally are resistant to this type of payment provision. Even where they are not, an employer likely will insist that such a provision be couched in terms of the 'prevailing' (or similar term) party being made whole for its costs by the losing party. That means 'what's good for the goose is good for the gander' – in any litigation between you and your employer in which either you sue or are sued by your employer for an alleged breach of some term of the separation agreement and you lose, you may be responsible for payment of your employer's counsel fees as well as your own.

The third, and most common option, of course, is to rely upon your employer's good faith. Cross your fingers, don't spend the severance before it is received, and pray that you are a good judge of character and your employer's good faith. Without intending to cast an undue shadow over this third – and probably most likely option – it should not go unsaid that such assumptions may well fly in the face of your assumptions before you started down this path: that your employer treated you poorly, unjustly and unfairly. Oh well.

Bon chance!

Made in United States
North Haven, CT
23 March 2023